A VIEW FROM THE BRIDGE

A View from the Bridge is a tragedy of a strong man who destroys himself in a clash between his blind passions and the primeval ideas of his own people about right living.

Eddie Carbone is an Italian longshoreman working in the New York docks. When his wife's cousins, Marco and Rodolpho, seek refuge as illegal immigrants from Sicily, Eddie agrees to shelter them. Trouble begins when his wife's niece Catherine, whom he has brought up with a possessive love which he does not understand, is attracted to the glamorous younger brother Rodolpho; and it culminates in baffled jealousy which drives him to commit an unforgivable crime against his family and the Sicilian community.

Although there could be no justification of the things Eddie does, his inevitable end evokes sympathy and a kind of awe.

D1442682

THE HEREFORD PLAYS

General Editor: E. R. Wood

Arthur Miller

A View from the Bridge

with an introduction by
E. R. WOOD

HEINEMANN
EDUCATIONAL

Heinemann Educational Books Ltd
Halley Court, Jordan Hill, Oxford OX2 8EJ

OXFORD   LONDON   EDINBURGH
MADRID   ATHENS   BOLOGNA   PARIS
MELBOURNE   SYDNEY   AUCKLAND
IBADAN   NAIROBI   HARARE   GABORONE
SINGAPORE   TOKYO   PORTSMOUTH NH (USA)

ISBN 0 435 22579 0

Introduction © E. R. Wood 1975
First published in Hereford Plays Series 1975

93 94 95 19 18 17 16 15 14

Printed in England by Clays Ltd, St Ives plc

Contents

CAST OF
THE FIRST LONDON PERFORMANCE

A View From The Bridge received its first production (in its present revised form) at the Comedy Theatre, London, on 11 October 1956. The cast was as follows:

LOUIS	Richard Harris
MIKE	Norman Mitchell
ALFIERI	Michael Gwynn
EDDIE	Anthony Quayle
CATHERINE	Mary Ure
BEATRICE	Megs Jenkins
MARCO	Ian Bannen
TONY	Ralph Nossek
RODOLPHO	Brian Bedford
FIRST IMMIGRATION OFFICER	John Stone
SECOND IMMIGRATION OFFICER	Colin Rix
MR LIPARI	Mervyn Blake
MRS LIPARI	Catherine Willmer
A 'SUBMARINE'	Peter James

The play was directed by Peter Brook

INTRODUCTION

ARTHUR MILLER was born in New York in 1915. His family were of Austrian Jewish origin, but the Jewish element does not appear to have been important in his upbringing. The Millers were prosperous manufacturers until they were ruined in the economic crisis which hit America in 1931. Thereafter, Arthur Miller grew up in poverty; he worked as an errand-boy in early mornings before going to school, where he did not distinguish himself. (His teachers could not remember him later.) After working for two years in an automobile parts warehouse, he had earned enough money to be able to enter the University of Michigan, where he helped to maintain himself by various jobs. Working at different times as a waiter, a factory hand and a lorry driver has given him plenty of experience of hardship and adversity.

He entered the University to study economics and history, but he also took a course in playwriting. After graduating in 1938 he made a living by writing radio scripts, and he completed a dozen plays that were never produced. His first Broadway play, *The Man who Had All the Luck* (1944) ran for only a week, but his next three established him as a major dramatist. They were *All My Sons* (1947), *Death of a Salesman* (1949) and *The Crucible* (1953) (all published in the Hereford Series). *A View from the Bridge* was presented in its original form, together with *A Memory of Two Mondays*, in 1955. *Incident at Vichy* and *After the Fall* followed in 1965, and *The Price* in 1968. His first comedy, *Creation of the World and Other Business*, was presented on Broadway in 1973. His work for the theatre has a world-wide reputation.

Private Lives and Social Plays

On Social Plays is the title of an essay by Arthur Miller on the concern he has shown in all his plays with man's responsibility as a social being, not merely as an individual interesting for his uniqueness.

One of the benefits offered by literature in general is a widening of awareness, an extension of our experience to the lives of other people. Usually we recognize some kinship with those others, and even enjoy living their lives in imagination, sharing their hopes and fears, their triumphs and troubles. But sometimes the gap is too wide. You could conceive, for example, of a story about a deaf and dumb mental defective or a gifted drop-out who wilfully brings misery on himself and all around him, though you might think you had nothing in common that would allow you to 'connect'. In the novel or short story form such a theme might be acceptable if it was convincing enough to enlarge your sympathies and arouse your interest in eccentricity and oddity.

Even in the theatre, eccentricity and oddity, and highly individual emotions and interests, are nowadays expected to hold the attention of playgoers. Is there any reason why not? Its traditions were otherwise. The ancient Greeks thought of the theatre as a place where the whole community came together and responded collectively to a spectacle that concerned them all – Man trying to come to terms with his Universe. So although the tragic hero was a particular individual in a particular set of circumstances – Oedipus or Orestes or Agamemnon caught up in a particular destiny – he seemed to stand for Mankind. Even in Shakespeare, though the hero may be beset with individual troubles not our own (Mother married to Uncle who murdered Father, for instance), we hear him speak of the ills that all flesh is heir to, and feel that his downfall is of universal significance. In more modern times audiences came to expect more individuality in principal characters, but they still expected a play to be more than a private matter. The playgoer would 'identify' with the 'hero' as a victim, no longer of Fate in the Greek sense, but of some power that determined his life, such as economic forces, or heredity, or psychological make-up, or Society itself. Such forces we are all involved in.

It may be that there is something essentially inappropriate in the presentation before a public assembly of completely private preoccupations, but the result may be an enlargement of the sensibilities of the audience and certainly a challenge welcomed by actors to extend the range of their art.

Now Arthur Miller has firmly expressed views on the scope and responsibilities of the theatre. He wants plays to deal with individuals, imagined in the details of their psychological make-up and their private circumstances; but he doesn't find this enough: he wants a sense of wider significance such as the Greeks achieved. 'The prime business of a play,' he has written in the introduction to the *Collected Plays*, 'is to arouse the passions of its audience so that by the route of passion may be opened up new relationships between man and men, and between men and Man.' In his essay *On Social Plays* he writes with approval of the Greek dramatists' concern with Man as a social animal rather than a separate entity, and of the preoccupation with Ultimate Law, 'Drama gains in weight,' he writes, 'as it deals with more and more of the whole man, not either his subjective or his social life alone, and the Greek was unable to conceive of man as anything except as a whole.'

A View from the Bridge

So *A View from the Bridge* is about the private life of Eddie Carbone, but at the same time about man as a social being. It is elemental, like a Greek tragedy, a story of self-destruction that is inevitable when a man of strong will defies the standards of right held by the people he belongs to.

Of course, the individual is imagined in psychological detail, presenting his motives, conscious and unconscious, in his relations with his wife Beatrice, his niece Catherine, and the people around. A skeleton outline of the plot may be useful as a preliminary to closer consideration.

Eddie Carbone is a docker living in a slum near Brooklyn Bridge. He has brought up as his daughter the girl Catherine, who is now old enough to go out to work and to attract the attention of the young men as she walks down the street. Eddie loves her with a fanatical possessiveness which he doesn't understand. He would like to keep her a child, unchanging. Into this household come two Sicilian cousins of Beatrice, illegal immigrants whose presence must be kept secret from the Immigration authorities. Eddie gets on well at first with the elder brother, Marco, whose whole interest is to earn money to send home to his wife and family in Sicily, but he instantly disapproves of Rodolpho, who is young, unmarried, and obviously attractive to

Catherine. Jealousy, contempt and frustration combine to make him desperate to destroy Rodolpho, and he finally denounces both the brothers (incidentally betraying two other illegal immigrants) to the Immigration authorities. For such betrayal there can be no forgiveness in a community so dependent on solidarity against the Law, and Marco kills him.

The lawyer Alfieri, who is both inside the action, and commenting on it from the outside, talks of the inevitability of Eddie's tragedy: 'I could see every step coming, step after step like a dark figure walking down a hall towards a certain door. I knew where he was heading for. I knew where he was going to end.'

Eddie's fate comes from a combination of his particular personality and the special community in which he lives. Being the kind of man he is, and involved in a community of Italian and Sicilian immigrants, he has no scope for managing his problem. The two factors are interwoven. His mind is fairly primitive; he doesn't understand his own feelings, and he disguises them from himself. (Miller made it clear in *All My Sons* that people manage their lives by lying to themselves.) Thus he uses his strait-laced Italian standards for women to justify his jealous restrictions on Catherine. Because of his puritanism he is genuinely shocked and appalled at the suggestion that his own interest in Catherine is not purely avuncular: 'That's what you think of me – that I could have such thoughts?'

Because he is intellectually limited he acts by instinct and prejudice. He is quite comic in his attempt to explain and justify his suspicions of Rodolpho – protesting that he has fair hair, a high singing voice, a taste for feminine occupations such as cooking and dress-making. It is all summed up in the conviction that Rodolpho is a homosexual, and therefore not a suitable husband (but who would be?) for Catherine. Eddie is most at home in action on a physical level – a big, strong, impulsive man.

The Italian or Sicilian element is of the essence of the situation. He and the people around him are not sophisticated Americans. They are immigrants, bringing with them the primitive way of life of Calabria or Sicily, both in its primeval virtues and its elemental brutal lawlessness. They are poor and hard-working, knowing what it is to starve. They care about the family and their responsibilities within it. They 'have respect' for women and think strictness a virtue. Eddie has a primitive man's views of the purposes for which marriage was ordained, and cannot believe that United States law will allow a young girl to be married to a man who, he suspects, 'ain't right.'

'Justice is very important here,' says Alfieri, ironically, for he means a rough Sicilian justice – nothing to do with the Law. They will all work together with 'the syndicate' to frustrate the Immigration laws, and betrayal of the common loyalty, such as Eddie commits, must be avenged by the methods of the vendetta. It could all have happened the same any time in the last two thousand years.

Yet it would be a mistake to over-emphasize the extent to which Eddie is a product of his environment and his origins. Arthur Miller does not accept wholly the idea, common in twentieth-century drama, of 'Man as a nearly passive creation of environment and family-created psychological drives.' He thinks that such determinism is incompatible with drama, because it excludes the all-important Will. So he thinks that a play must strike a balance which embraces both determinism and the paradox of will. 'We are made and yet are more than what made us.'

So we must salute in Eddie a strong and defiant will that is his own, and recognition of this leads us on to another favourite yet often fatal quality in Miller's heroes – the fact that they cannot or will not 'settle for half'. Most of us do settle for half rather than destroy ourselves, and, as Alfieri says at the end of the play, 'it is better to settle for half – it *must* be' (especially when you are in the wrong). Yet the man who is purely himself, who goes all out, who will not compromise, demands respect, even awe. At the end Eddie does not gain our admiration exactly, because what he has done is indefensible and he will not admit it, but there is a certain wonder in it.

Like other heroes of Miller's plays, Eddie cares deeply about his 'Name', even when he has lost it irrevocably. This is more than mere reputation – what others think and say of him; it is his own sense of himself, his integrity. 'How may I live without my name?' asks John Proctor in *The Crucible*; and he goes to his death rather than lose it. Eddie's name was already lost. He could have saved his life; he could have accepted Rodolpho's solution, accepted a sort of apology from the man he had most wronged, and pretended to be reconciled, so stealing Marco's thunder. But this would have been to 'settle for half'. Instead he went on insisting that Marco must 'give him back his name'. He is guilty and must know he is guilty. There is no honourable way out but to die. To be a tragic hero, you do not have to be in the right; you have to be true to yourself.

Dramatic qualities

Arthur Miller values the traditional virtues of the firmly constructed play which develops the essence of the conflict in exciting well-shaped clashes; but he is interested in experiment, in varying the orthodox realistic forms. This play is apparently a little looser in construction than some, moving along almost casually with its narrator who fills in the gaps and takes part quite easily in the action when required, and its scenes that sometimes fade out rather quietly on an anti-climax; but there is really nothing loose or casual: the play is much more tautly organized than it seems. Every scene makes its point firmly, and the tension is sustained in a pattern that reflects the sense of inevitability in Eddie's tragedy.

From the opening scene we are conscious of the friction in the Carbone household, arising from Eddie's possessiveness about Catherine which must trouble his wife, his unwillingness to let her grow up and away from him. The talk of illegal immigrants naturally brings up the fate of Vinny Bolzano, who snitched to the Immigration, and what his family did to him. 'You'll never see him again, a guy do a thing like that?' says Eddie with unconscious dramatic irony, unknowingly preparing the audience for the enormity of his own crime and the revulsion of the whole community. The arrival of Marco and Rodolpho is simple and quiet, but Catherine's reactions to the younger man create from the first a sensitive spot; and Eddie soon begins to exclude Rodolpho from the conversation. He stops him, ostensibly on security grounds that are reasonable but not the real motive, when he begins to show how he can sing. From now on, every turn in the dialogue is a thrust or parry in the under-the-surface fight, so that even so slight a matter as Catherine's attentiveness in putting sugar into Rodolpho's coffee brings the scene to an end on a minor defeat for the troubled Eddie.

The next scene develops the three-cornered conflict and ends in Beatrice telling Catherine firmly that she must break free. Then the essence of Eddie's trouble is explored in the talk with Alfieri, who sums up: 'The child has to grow up and go away, and the man has to learn to forget – what other way can it end? . . . She wants to get married, Eddie. She can't marry you, can she?' Alfieri's advice is pure reason, put to Eddie with sympathy and understanding. But reason is no good to Eddie.

In a later passage of arms in the home Eddie is capable of using reason as a weapon for himself, and scoring points. 'If he's here to work,' he argues, 'then he should work; if he's here for a good time then he could fool around. But I understood, Marco, that you was both coming to make a living for your family.' But the sparring with words is then supplemented by physical action. Catherine hits at Eddie by inviting Rodolpho to dance with her. Eddie counters by giving him a lesson in boxing. This is no crude beating up; Eddie pretends to be pleased with his pupil's progress; but the real hostility is ill-concealed beneath the show of friendly encouragement and at the end the motive is evident to Rodolpho, though he protests that he was not hurt – only surprised – by a hard blow. Marco, silently watching, is not for a moment deceived. As Rodolpho resumes dancing with Catherine, Marco initiates a contest in physical strength – the chair-lifting challenge – and the result is a defeat for Eddie, as the chair is raised by Marco like a weapon over his head. So we have had a series of bouts in the visual language of theatre action, at the conclusion of which Marco plainly says to Eddie – though not in words – 'You think you are strong; you have shown that you can knock Rodolpho about; but if it comes to a fight with me, I can kill you.' And there the act ends in a foreshadowing of what is to come.

Marco's emergence as a potential enemy of Eddie is important at that point; for the main conflict moves in the second act to Eddie and Marco. When Eddie commits the unforgivable crime, it is Marco who is the implacable avenger. It is Marco we remember breaking away from the arresting officer to spit at Eddie, and it is Marco whose ringing challenge in the last moments chills the spine, as he calls from outside, 'Eddie Carbone!', then facing him with all the contempt of a Sicilian for a man who would betray another to the Law – 'Animal! You go on your knees to me!' Strong drama indeed! But it is not mere theatricality; it presents in theatrical terms the core of the play's meaning. Eddie's destruction is inevitable, for he has betrayed his own sense of right.

His death in Beatrice's arms, reconciled to the two women (who seem to be giving him back his 'name' as they call it again and again) may seem like a sentimental end at variance with the play's stark truth, but their love and grief for him is consistent with Alfieri's final comment (which is perhaps the author's own) – 'Even as I know how wrong he was . . . I confess that something perversely pure calls to me from his memory.' Love for our fellows, and mourning for the death of a loved one, is not necessarily in proportion to the marks we would give them for good conduct.

Language

A View from the Bridge was originally written as a one-act play, first produced in New York in 1955. It was not very successful, and Arthur Miller rewrote and expanded it for the London production by Peter Brook the following year. One of the interesting changes was in the language. The first version contained a good deal that was printed as verse, including passages retained in the present edition but printed as prose. Verse seemed to suit the speeches of Alfieri where he took on – and still retains – some of the character of a Greek Chorus, placing the action of the play outside the confines of specific time and place.

> And yet, when the tide is right,
> And the green smell of the sea
> Floats through my window,
> I must look up at the circling pigeons of the poor,
> And I see falcons there,
> And the hunting eagles of the olden time,
> Fierce above Italian forests. . . .

> And as the parties tell me what the trouble is
> I see cobwebs tearing, Adriatic ruins rebuilding themselves, Calabria;
> The eyes of the plaintiff seem suddenly carved,
> His voice booming toward me over many fallen stones.

So Alfieri is no longer solely the New York lawyer hearing the twentieth-century troubles of local litigants, but a listener outside time aware of the heritage of their classical ancestry. The heightened speech, with its imagery of the heroic past, is appropriate. Of course, when Alfieri takes up his role in the affairs of Eddie and Marco, he speaks a plain, direct language to be expected of a lawyer.

Eddie, as has been said, is no intellectual, and at times has no words to express his emotions, but must do so in impulsive action. For example, at a crisis when he tells Rodolpho to pack up and get out, he seizes Catherine and kisses her on the mouth, thus avowing more than he himself understands or could ever put into words. A few moments afterwards, when Rodolpho in fury has attacked him, he answers with the unspeakable insult of a kiss on his lips, an assertion that Catherine understands with such horror that 'she goes around shaking all the time; she can't sleep.'

But Eddie is very far from being inarticulate: indeed, he often shows a turn of phrase that is marvellously vivid and economical. He is especially eloquent on the subject of Rodolpho, who 'gives him the heeby-jeebies' from the first:

'He's a blond guy . . . like . . . platinum . . . I mean if you close the paper fast, you could blow him over.'

'What does he do with his first money? A snappy new jacket he buys, records, a pointy pair new shoes and his brother's kids are starving over there with tuberculosis.'

'He could be picked up any day here and he's back pushing taxis up the hill.'

'Even a mouse, if you catch a teeny mouse and hold it in your hand, that mouse can give you the right kind of fight. He didn't give me the right kind of fight.'

'You marry him and the next time you see him it'll be for divorce.'

His picture of life with Beatrice is perhaps unfair, but lively:

'The last year or two I come in the house I don't know what's gonna hit me. It's a shootin' gallery and I'm the pigeon.'

The two immigrants, though they both have the advantage of a foreign turn of speech, are sharply contrasted. Marco is laconic, hardly speaking in sentences: Rodolpho is eloquent, with a kind of poetry. (His lines about what a life he could lead back home if he had a blue motor-cycle were originally printed as verse.) Notice how he can describe the essence of his situation with effective metaphor and urgent rhythm:

'Do you think I am so desperate? My brother is desperate, not me. You think I would carry on my back the rest of my life a woman I didn't love, just to be an American? It's so wonderful? You think we have no tall buildings in Italy? Electric lights? No wide streets? No flags? No automobiles? Only work we don't have. I want to be an American so I can work, that is the only wonder here – work!'

In his talk with Catherine he is able to say things (like 'My heart dies to look at you') which might sound sentimental in an Englishman or a tough American, but sound right for him, and he brings out in her a touch of poetry too. She is able to describe to him the quality of her love for Eddie (for it *is* true love):

> 'I can tell a block away when he's blue in his mind and just wants to talk to somebody quiet and nice ... I can tell when he's hungry or wants a beer before he even says anything. I know when his feet hurt him, I mean I *know* him, and now I'm supposed to turn around and make a stranger of him?'

Most of the dialogue of the play is naturalistic American talk, sometimes with an immigrant flavour, but it has all the American vigour it needs, with the capacity to rise to the demands of emotion. After an appraisal of the dialogue of the greater part of the play, it is specially interesting to look back at the original version of the concluding lines, and to consider what was gained or lost by scrapping it and substituting the result of the author's second thoughts. Here is Alfieri speaking at the end of the play as it was first presented:

> Most of the time now we settle for half,
> And I like it better.
> And yet, when the tide is right
> And the green smell of the sea
> Floats in through my window,
> The waves of this bay
> Are the waves against Siracusa,
> And I see a face that suddenly seems carved;
> The eyes look like tunnels
> Leading back toward some ancestral beach
> Where all of us once lived.
> And I wonder at those times
> How much all of us
> Really lives there yet,
> And when we will truly have moved on,
> On and away from that dark place,
> That world that has fallen to stones?
> This is the end of the story. Goodnight.

You will see that this rejected ending repeats ideas already expressed and uses again lines which evidently pleased the playwright, but it does not clarify Alfieri's feelings about Eddie's tragedy. It is perhaps more appropriate to the title. The title has a double suggestion: the Bridge can be Brooklyn Bridge, near which the events are worked out, or a position of detachment (as on a ship) from which events can be observed. In the version printed above, Alfieri seems to assume such a position of detachment; but in the revised version he is personally involved. The intention, as well as the tone, is quite different.

FOR FURTHER STUDY

Collected Plays (Cresset Press, 1958) contains *All My Sons, Death of a Salesman, The Crucible, A Memory of Two Mondays* and *A View from the Bridge*, with a long and important Introduction by the author.

The original one-act version of *A View from the Bridge* is published in New York by the Viking Press (1955).

All My Sons, Death of a Salesman and *The Crucible* are available in the Hereford Series (Heinemann Educational Books) with Introductions by E. R. Wood.

All these plays, as well as *After the Fall* and *The Price* are published by Penguin books.

Arthur Miller: The Burning Glass by Sheila Huftel (W. H. Allen, 1965) examines all the plays up to (but not including) *The Price*.

Arthur Miller by Ronald Hayman (Heinemann Educational Books, 1970) includes an account of *The Price*.

Arthur Miller, by Dennis Welland (Oliver and Boyd, 1961) takes the reader as far as *A View from the Bridge*.

THE CHARACTERS

LOUIS

MIKE

ALFIERI

EDDIE

CATHERINE

BEATRICE

MARCO

TONY

RODOLPHO

FIRST IMMIGRATION OFFICER

SECOND IMMIGRATION OFFICER

MR LIPARI

MRS LIPARI

TWO 'SUBMARINES'

NEIGHBOURS

A VIEW
FROM THE BRIDGE

A VIEW FROM THE BRIDGE

ACT ONE

The street and house front of a tenement building. The front is skeletal entirely. The main acting area is the living room–dining room of Eddie's apartment. It is a worker's flat, clean, sparse, homely. There is a rocker down front; a round dining table at center, with chairs; and a portable phonograph.

At back are a bedroom door and an opening to the kitchen; none of these interiors are seen.

At the right, forestage, a desk. This is Mr. Alfieri's law office.

There is also a telephone booth. This is not used until the last scenes, so it may be covered or left in view.

A stairway leads up to the apartment, and then farther up to the next story, which is not seen.

Ramps, representing the street, run upstage and off to right and left.

As the curtain rises, Louis and Mike, longshoremen, are pitching coins against the building at left.

A distant foghorn blows.

Enter Alfieri, a lawyer in his fifties turning gray; he is portly, good-humored, and thoughtful. The two pitchers nod to him as he passes. He crosses the stage to his desk, removes his hat, runs his fingers through his hair, and grinning, speaks to the audience.

ALFIERI: You wouldn't have known it, but something amusing has just happened. You see how uneasily they nod to me? That's because I am a lawyer. In this neighborhood to meet a lawyer or a priest on the street is unlucky. We're only thought of in connection with disasters, and they'd rather not get too close.

I often think that behind that suspicious little nod of theirs lie three thousand years of distrust. A lawyer means the law, and in Sicily, from where their fathers came, the law has not been a friendly idea since the Greeks were beaten.

I am inclined to notice the ruins in things, perhaps because I was born in Italy. . . . I only came here when I was twenty-five. In those days, Al Capone, the greatest Carthaginian of all, was learning his trade on these pavements, and Frankie Yale himself was cut precisely in half by a machine gun on the corner of Union Street, two blocks away. Oh, there were many here who were justly shot by unjust men. Justice is very important here.

But this is Red Hook, not Sicily. This is the slum that faces the bay on the seaward side of Brooklyn Bridge. This is the gullet of New York swallowing the tonnage of the world. And now we are quite civilized, quite American. Now we settle for half, and I like it better. I no longer keep a pistol in my filing cabinet.

And my practice is entirely unromantic.

My wife has warned me, so have my friends; they tell me the people in this neighborhood lack elegance, glamour. After all, who have I dealt with in my life? Longshoremen and their wives, and fathers and grandfathers, compensation cases, evictions, family squabbles—the petty troubles of the poor—and yet . . . every few years there is still a case, and as the parties tell me what the trouble is, the flat air in my office suddenly washes in with the green scent of the sea, the dust in this air is blown away and the thought comes that in some Caesar's year, in Calabria perhaps or on the cliff at Syracuse, another lawyer, quite differently dressed, heard the same complaint and sat there as powerless as I, and watched it run its bloody course.

Eddie has appeared and has been pitching coins with the men and is highlighted among them. He is forty—a husky, slightly overweight longshoreman.

This one's name was Eddie Carbone, a longshoreman working the docks from Brooklyn Bridge to the breakwater where the open sea begins.

Alfieri walks into darkness.

EDDIE, *moving up steps into doorway:* Well, I'll see ya, fellas.

Catherine enters from kitchen, crosses down to window, looks out.

LOUIS: You workin' tomorrow?

EDDIE: Yeah, there's another day yet on that ship. See ya, Louis.

Eddie goes into the house, as light rises in the apartment.

Catherine is waving to Louis from the window and turns to him.

CATHERINE: Hi, Eddie!

Eddie is pleased and therefore shy about it; he hangs up his cap and jacket.

EDDIE: Where you goin' all dressed up?

CATHERINE, *running her hands over her skirt:* I just got it. You like it?

EDDIE: Yeah, it's nice. And what happened to your hair?

CATHERINE: You like it? I fixed it different. *Calling to kitchen:* He's here, B.!

EDDIE: Beautiful. Turn around, lemme see in the back. *She turns for him.* Oh, if your mother was alive to see you now! She wouldn't believe it.

CATHERINE: You like it, huh?

EDDIE: You look like one of them girls that went to college. Where you goin'?

CATHERINE, *taking his arm:* Wait'll B. comes in, I'll tell you something. Here, sit down. *She is walking him to the armchair. Calling offstage:* Hurry up, will you, B.?

EDDIE, *sitting:* What's goin' on?

CATHERINE: I'll get you a beer, all right?

EDDIE: Well, tell me what happened. Come over here, talk to me.

CATHERINE: I want to wait till B. comes in. *She sits on her heels beside him.* Guess how much we paid for the skirt.

EDDIE: I think it's too short, ain't it?

CATHERINE, *standing:* No! not when I stand up.

EDDIE: Yeah, but you gotta sit down sometimes.

CATHERINE: Eddie, it's the style now. *She walks to show him.* I mean, if you see me walkin' down the street—

EDDIE: Listen, you been givin' me the willies the way you walk down the street, I mean it.

CATHERINE: Why?

EDDIE: Catherine, I don't want to be a pest, but I'm tellin' you you're walkin' wavy.

CATHERINE: I'm walkin' wavy?

EDDIE: Now don't aggravate me, Katie, you are walkin' wavy! I don't like the looks they're givin' you in the candy store. And with them new high heels on the sidewalk—clack, clack, clack. The heads are turnin' like windmills.

CATHERINE: But those guys look at all the girls, you know that.

EDDIE: You ain't "all the girls."

CATHERINE, *almost in tears because he disapproves:* What do you want me to do? You want me to—

EDDIE: Now don't get mad, kid.

CATHERINE: Well, I don't know what you want from me.

EDDIE: Katie, I promised your mother on her deathbed. I'm responsible for you. You're a baby, you don't understand these things. I mean like when you stand here by the window, wavin' outside.

CATHERINE: I was wavin' to Louis!

EDDIE: Listen, I could tell you things about Louis which you wouldn't wave to him no more.

CATHERINE, *trying to joke him out of his warning:* Eddie, I wish there was one guy you couldn't tell me things about!

EDDIE: Catherine, do me a favor, will you? You're gettin' to be a big girl now, you gotta keep yourself more, you can't be so friendly, kid. *Calls:* Hey, B., what're you doin' in there? *To Catherine:* Get her in here, will you? I got news for her.

CATHERINE, *starting out:* What?

EDDIE: Her cousins landed.

CATHERINE, *clapping her hands together:* No! *She turns instantly and starts for the kitchen.* B.! Your cousins!

    Beatrice enters, wiping her hands with a towel.

BEATRICE, *in the face of Catherine's shout:* What?

CATHERINE: Your cousins got in!

BEATRICE, *astounded, turns to Eddie:* What are you talkin' about? Where?

EDDIE: I was just knockin' off work before and Tony Bereli come over to me; he says the ship is in the North River.

BEATRICE—*her hands are clasped at her breast; she seems half in fear, half in unutterable joy:* They're all right?

EDDIE: He didn't see them yet, they're still on board. But as soon as they get off he'll meet them. He figures about ten o'clock they'll be here.

BEATRICE *sits, almost weak from tension:* And they'll let them off the ship all right? That's fixed, heh?

EDDIE: Sure, they give them regular seamen papers and they walk off with the crew. Don't worry about it, B., there's nothin' to it. Couple of hours they'll be here.

BEATRICE: What happened? They wasn't supposed to be till next Thursday.

EDDIE: I don't know; they put them on any ship they can get them out on. Maybe the other ship they was supposed to take there was some danger— What you cryin' about?

BEATRICE, *astounded and afraid:* I'm— I just—I can't believe it! I didn't even buy a new table cloth; I was gonna wash the walls—

EDDIE: Listen, they'll think it's a millionaire's house compared to the way they live. Don't worry about the walls. They'll be thankful. *To Catherine:* Whyn't you run down buy a table cloth. Go ahead, here. *He is reaching into his pocket.*

CATHERINE: There's no stores open now.

EDDIE, *to Beatrice:* You was gonna put a new cover on the chair.

BEATRICE: I know—well, I thought it was gonna be next week! I was gonna clean the walls, I was gonna wax the floors. *She stands disturbed.*

CATHERINE, *pointing upward:* Maybe Mrs. Dondero upstairs—

BEATRICE, *of the table cloth:* No, hers is worse than this one. *Suddenly:* My God, I don't even have nothin' to eat for them! *She starts for the kitchen.*

EDDIE, *reaching out and grabbing her arm:* Hey, hey! Take it easy.

BEATRICE: No, I'm just nervous, that's all. *To Catherine:* I'll make the fish.

EDDIE: You're savin' their lives, what're you worryin' about the table cloth? They probably didn't see a table cloth in their whole life where they come from.

BEATRICE, *looking into his eyes:* I'm just worried about you, that's all I'm worried.

EDDIE: Listen, as long as they know where they're gonna sleep.

BEATRICE: I told them in the letters. They're sleepin' on the floor.

EDDIE: Beatrice, all I'm worried about is you got such a heart that I'll end up on the floor with you, and they'll be in our bed.

BEATRICE: All right, stop it.

EDDIE: Because as soon as you see a tired relative, I end up on the floor.

BEATRICE: When did you end up on the floor?

EDDIE: When your father's house burned down I didn't end up on the floor?

BEATRICE: Well, their house burned down!

EDDIE: Yeah, but it didn't keep burnin' for two weeks!

BEATRICE: All right, look, I'll tell them to go someplace else. *She starts into the kitchen.*

EDDIE: Now wait a minute. Beatrice! *She halts. He goes to her.* I just don't want you bein' pushed around, that's all. You got too big a heart. *He touches her hand.* What're you so touchy?

BEATRICE: I'm just afraid if it don't turn out good you'll be mad at me.

EDDIE: Listen, if everybody keeps his mouth shut, nothin' can happen. They'll pay for their board.

BEATRICE: Oh, I told them.

EDDIE: Then what the hell. *Pause. He moves.* It's an honor, B. I mean it. I was just thinkin' before, comin' home, suppose my father didn't come to this country, and I was starvin' like them over there . . . and I had people in America could keep me a couple of months? The man would be honored to lend me a place to sleep.

BEATRICE—*there are tears in her eyes. She turns to Catherine:* You see what he is? *She turns and grabs Eddie's face in her hands.* Mmm! You're an angel! God'll bless you. *He is gratefully smiling.* You'll see, you'll get a blessing for this!

EDDIE, *laughing:* I'll settle for my own bed.

BEATRICE: Go, Baby, set the table.

CATHERINE: We didn't tell him about me yet.

BEATRICE: Let him eat first, then we'll tell him. Bring everything in. *She hurries Catherine out.*

EDDIE, *sitting at the table:* What's all that about? Where's she goin'?

BEATRICE: Noplace. It's very good news, Eddie. I want you to be happy.

EDDIE: What's goin' on?

Catherine enters with plates, forks.

BEATRICE: She's got a job.

Pause. Eddie looks at Catherine, then back to Beatrice.

EDDIE: What job? She's gonna finish school.

CATHERINE: Eddie, you won't believe it—

EDDIE: No—no, you gonna finish school. What kinda job, what do you mean? All of a sudden you—

CATHERINE: Listen a minute, it's wonderful.

EDDIE: It's not wonderful. You'll never get nowheres unless you finish school. You can't take no job. Why didn't you ask me before you take a job?

BEATRICE: She's askin' you now, she didn't take nothin' yet.

CATHERINE: Listen a minute! I came to school this morning and the principal called me out of the class, see? To go to his office.

EDDIE: Yeah?

CATHERINE: So I went in and he says to me he's got my records, y'know? And there's a company wants a girl right away. It ain't exactly a secretary, it's a stenographer first, but pretty soon you get to be secretary. And he says to me that I'm the best student in the whole class—

BEATRICE: You hear that?

EDDIE: Well why not? Sure she's the best.

CATHERINE: I'm the best student, he says, and if I want, I should take the job and the end of the year he'll let me take the examination and he'll give me the certificate. So I'll save practically a year!

EDDIE, *strangely nervous:* Where's the job? What company?

CATHERINE: It's a big plumbing company over Nostrand Avenue.

EDDIE: Nostrand Avenue and where?

CATHERINE: It's someplace by the Navy Yard.

BEATRICE: Fifty dollars a week, Eddie.

EDDIE, *to Catherine, surprised:* Fifty?

CATHERINE: I swear.

Pause.

EDDIE: What about all the stuff you wouldn't learn this year, though?

CATHERINE: There's nothin' more to learn, Eddie, I just gotta practice from now on. I know all the symbols and I know the keyboard. I'll just get faster, that's all. And when I'm workin' I'll keep gettin' better and better, you see?

BEATRICE: Work is the best practice anyway.

EDDIE: That ain't what I wanted, though.

CATHERINE: Why! It's a great big company—

EDDIE: I don't like that neighborhood over there.

CATHERINE: It's a block and half from the subway, he says.

EDDIE: Near the Navy Yard plenty can happen in a block and a half. And a plumbin' company! That's one step over the water front. They're practically longshoremen.

BEATRICE: Yeah, but she'll be in the office, Eddie.

EDDIE: I know she'll be in the office, but that ain't what I had in mind.

BEATRICE: Listen, she's gotta go to work sometime.

EDDIE: Listen, B., she'll be with a lotta plumbers? And sailors up and down the street? So what did she go to school for?

CATHERINE: But it's fifty a week, Eddie.

EDDIE: Look, did I ask you for money? I supported you this long I support you a little more. Please, do me a favor, will ya? I want you to be with different kind of people. I want you to be in a nice office. Maybe a lawyer's office someplace in New York in one of them nice buildings. I mean if you're gonna get outa here then get out; don't go practically in the same kind of neighborhood.

Pause. Catherine lowers her eyes.

BEATRICE: Go, Baby, bring in the supper. *Catherine goes out.* Think about it a little bit, Eddie. Please. She's crazy to start work. It's not a little shop, it's a big company. Some day she could be a secretary. They picked her out of the whole class. *He is silent, staring down at the tablecloth, fingering the pattern.* What are you worried about? She could take care of herself. She'll get out of the subway and be in the office in two minutes.

EDDIE, *somehow sickened:* I know that neighborhood, B., I don't like it.

BEATRICE: Listen, if nothin' happened to he\
it ain't gonna happen noplace else. *She turns h*\
you gotta get used to it, she's no baby no more.\
He turns his head away. You hear me? *She is*\
understand you; she's seventeen years old, you go.\
the house all her life?

EDDIE, *insulted:* What kinda remark is that?

BEATRICE, *with sympathy but insistent force:* Well, I o ....er-
stand when it ends. First it was gonna be when she gradu..ed high
school, so she graduated high school. Then it was gonna be when
she learned stenographer, so she learned stenographer. So what're
we gonna wait for now? I mean it, Eddie, sometimes I don't
understand you; they picked her out of the whole class, it's an
honor for her.

    *Catherine enters with food, which she silently sets on the
table. After a moment of watching her face, Eddie breaks into a
smile, but it almost seems that tears will form in his eyes.*

EDDIE: With your hair that way you look like a madonna, you
know that? You're the madonna type. *She doesn't look at him, but
continues ladling out food onto the plates.* You wanna go to work,
heh, Madonna?

CATHERINE, *softly:* Yeah.

EDDIE, *with a sense of her childhood, her babyhood, and the years:*
All right, go to work. *She looks at him, then rushes and hugs him.*
Hey, hey! Take it easy! *He holds her face away from him to look
at her.* What're you cryin' about? *He is affected by her, but smiles
his emotion away.*

CATHERINE, *sitting at her place:* I just— *Bursting out:* I'm gonna
buy all new dishes with my first pay! *They laugh warmly.* I mean
it. I'll fix up the whole house! I'll buy a rug!

EDDIE: And then you'll move away.

CATHERINE: No, Eddie!

EDDIE, *grinning:* Why not? That's life. And you'll come visit on
Sundays, then once a month, then Christmas and New Year's,
finally.

CATHERINE, *grasping his arm to reassure him and to erase the
accusation:* No, please!

EDDIE, *smiling but hurt:* I only ask you one thing—don't trust oody. You got a good aunt but she's got too big a heart, you learned bad from her. Believe me.

BEATRICE: Be the way you are, Katie, don't listen to him.

EDDIE, *to Beatrice—strangely and quickly resentful:* You lived in a house all your life, what do you know about it? You never worked in your life.

BEATRICE: She likes people. What's wrong with that?

EDDIE: Because most people ain't people. She's goin' to work; plumbers; they'll chew her to pieces if she don't watch out. *To Catherine:* Believe me, Katie, the less you trust, the less you be sorry.

> *Eddie crosses himself and the women do the same, and they eat.*

CATHERINE: First thing I'll buy is a rug, heh, B.?

BEATRICE: I don't mind. *To Eddie:* I smelled coffee all day today. You unloadin' coffee today?

EDDIE: Yeah, a Brazil ship.

CATHERINE: I smelled it too. It smelled all over the neighborhood.

EDDIE: That's one time, boy, to be a longshoreman is a pleasure. I could work coffee ships twenty hours a day. You go down in the hold, y'know? It's like flowers, that smell. We'll bust a bag tomorrow, I'll bring you some.

BEATRICE: Just be sure there's no spiders in it, will ya? I mean it. *She directs this to Catherine, rolling her eyes upward.* I still remember that spider coming out of that bag he brung home. I nearly died.

EDDIE: You call that a spider? You oughta see what comes outa the bananas sometimes.

BEATRICE: Don't talk about it!

EDDIE: I seen spiders could stop a Buick.

BEATRICE, *clapping her hands over her ears:* All right, shut up!

EDDIE, *laughing and taking a watch out of his pocket:* Well, who started with spiders?

BEATRICE: All right, I'm sorry, I didn't mean it. Just don't bring none home again. What time is it?

EDDIE: Quarter nine. *Puts watch back in his pocket.*

> *They continue eating in silence.*

CATHERINE: He's bringin' them ten o'clock, Tony?

EDDIE: Around, yeah. *He eats.*

CATHERINE: Eddie, suppose somebody asks if they're livin' here. *He looks at her as though already she had divulged something publicly. Defensively:* I mean if they ask.

EDDIE: Now look, Baby, I can see we're gettin' mixed up again here.

CATHERINE: No, I just mean . . . people'll see them goin' in and out.

EDDIE: I don't care who sees them goin' in and out as long as you don't see them goin' in and out. And this goes for you too, B. You don't see nothin' and you don't know nothin'.

BEATRICE: What do you mean? I understand.

EDDIE: You don't understand; you still think you can talk about this to somebody just a little bit. Now lemme say it once and for all, because you're makin' me nervous again, both of you. I don't care if somebody comes in the house and sees them sleepin' on the floor, it never comes out of your mouth who they are or what they're doin' here.

BEATRICE: Yeah, but my mother'll know—

EDDIE: Sure she'll know, but just don't you be the one who told her, that's all. This is the United States government you're playin' with now, this is the Immigration Bureau. If you said it you knew it, if you didn't say it you didn't know it.

CATHERINE: Yeah, but Eddie, suppose somebody—

EDDIE: I don't care what question it is. You—don't—know—nothin'. They got stool pigeons all over this neighborhood they're payin' them every week for information, and you don't know who they are. It could be your best friend. You hear? *To Beatrice:* Like Vinny Bolzano, remember Vinny?

BEATRICE: Oh, yeah. God forbid.

EDDIE: Tell her about Vinny. *To Catherine:* You think I'm blowin' steam here? *To Beatrice:* Go ahead, tell her. *To Catherine:* You was a baby then. There was a family lived next door to her mother, he was about sixteen—

BEATRICE: No, he was no more than fourteen, cause I was to his confirmation in Saint Agnes. But the family had an uncle that they were hidin' in the house, and he snitched to the Immigration.

CATHERINE: The kid snitched?

EDDIE: On his own uncle!

CATHERINE: What, was he crazy?

EDDIE: He was crazy after, I tell you that, boy.

BEATRICE: Oh, it was terrible. He had five brothers and the old father. And they grabbed him in the kitchen and pulled him down the stairs—three flights his head was bouncin' like a coconut. And they spit on him in the street, his own father and his brothers. The whole neighborhood was cryin'.

CATHERINE: Ts! So what happened to him?

BEATRICE: I think he went away. *To Eddie:* I never seen him again, did you?

EDDIE *rises during this, taking out his watch:* Him? You'll never see him no more, a guy do a thing like that? How's he gonna show his face? *To Catherine, as he gets up uneasily:* Just remember, kid, you can quicker get back a million dollars that was stole than a word that you gave away. *He is standing now, stretching his back.*

CATHERINE: Okay, I won't say a word to nobody, I swear.

EDDIE: Gonna rain tomorrow. We'll be slidin' all over the decks. Maybe you oughta put something on for them, they be here soon.

BEATRICE: I only got fish, I hate to spoil it if they ate already. I'll wait, it only takes a few minutes; I could broil it.

CATHERINE: What happens, Eddie, when that ship pulls out and they ain't on it, though? Don't the captain say nothin'?

EDDIE, *slicing an apple with his pocket knife:* Captain's pieced off, what do you mean?

CATHERINE: Even the captain?

EDDIE: What's the matter, the captain don't have to live? Captain gets a piece, maybe one of the mates, piece for the guy in Italy who fixed the papers for them, Tony here'll get a little bite. . . .

BEATRICE: I just hope they get work here, that's all I hope.

EDDIE: Oh, the syndicate'll fix jobs for them; till they pay 'em off they'll get them work every day. It's after the pay-off, then they'll have to scramble like the rest of us.

BEATRICE: Well, it be better than they got there.

EDDIE: Oh sure, well, listen. So you gonna start Monday, heh, Madonna?

CATHERINE, *embarrassed:* I'm supposed to, yeah.

Eddie is standing facing the two seated women. First Beatrice smiles, then Catherine, for a powerful emotion is on him, a childish one and a knowing fear, and the tears show in his eyes—and they are shy before the avowal.

EDDIE: *sadly smiling, yet somehow proud of her:* Well . . . I hope you have good luck. I wish you the best. You know that, kid.

CATHERINE, *rising, trying to laugh:* You sound like I'm goin' a million miles!

EDDIE: I know. I guess I just never figured on one thing.

CATHERINE, *smiling:* What?

EDDIE: That you would ever grow up. *He utters a soundless laugh at himself, feeling his breast pocket of his shirt.* I left a cigar in my other coat, I think. *He starts for the bedroom.*

CATHERINE: Stay there! I'll get it for you.

She hurries out. There is a slight pause, and Eddie turns to Beatrice, who has been avoiding his gaze.

EDDIE: What are you mad at me lately?

BEATRICE: Who's mad? *She gets up, clearing the dishes.* I'm not mad. *She picks up the dishes and turns to him.* You're the one is mad. *She turns and goes into the kitchen as Catherine enters from the bedroom with a cigar and a pack of matches.*

CATHERINE: Here! I'll light it for you! *She strikes a match and holds it to his cigar. He puffs. Quietly:* Don't worry about me, Eddie, heh?

EDDIE: Don't burn yourself. *Just in time she blows out the match.* You better go in help her with the dishes.

CATHERINE *turns quickly to the table, and, seeing the table cleared, she says, almost guiltily:* Oh! *She hurries into the kitchen, and as she exits there:* I'll do the dishes, B.!

Alone, Eddie stands looking toward the kitchen for a moment. Then he takes out his watch, glances at it, replaces it in his pocket, sits in the armchair, and stares at the smoke flowing out of his mouth.

The lights go down, then come up on Alfieri, who has moved onto the forestage.

ALFIERI: He was as good a man as he had to be in a life that was hard and even. He worked on the piers when there was work, he brought home his pay, and he lived. And toward ten o'clock of that night, after they had eaten, the cousins came.

The lights fade on Alfieri and rise on the street.

Enter Tony, escorting Marco and Rodolpho, each with a valise. Tony halts, indicates the house. They stand for a moment looking at it.

MARCO—*he is a square-built peasant of thirty-two, suspicious, tender, and quiet-voiced:* Thank you.

TONY: You're on your own now. Just be careful, that's all. Ground floor.

MARCO: Thank you.

TONY, *indicating the house:* I'll see you on the pier tomorrow. You'll go to work.

Marco nods. Tony continues on walking down the street.

RODOLPHO: This will be the first house I ever walked into in America! Imagine! She said they were poor!

MARCO: Ssh! Come. *They go to door.*

Marco knocks. The lights rise in the room. Eddie goes and opens the door. Enter Marco and Rodolpho, removing their caps. Beatrice and Catherine enter from the kitchen. The lights fade in the street.

EDDIE: You Marco?

MARCO: Marco.

EDDIE: Come on in! *He shakes Marco's hand.*

BEATRICE: Here, take the bags!

MARCO *nods, looks to the women and fixes on Beatrice. Crosses to Beatrice.* Are you my cousin?

She nods. He kisses her hand.

BEATRICE, *above the table, touching her chest with her hand:* Beatrice. This is my husband, Eddie. *All nod.* Catherine, my sister Nancy's daughter. *The Brothers nod.*

MARCO, *indicating Rodolpho:* My brother. Rodolpho. *Rodolpho nods. Marco comes with a certain formal stiffness to Eddie.* I want to tell you now Eddie—when you say go, we will go.

EDDIE: Oh, no . . . *Takes Marco's bag.*

MARCO: I see it's a small house, but soon, maybe, we can have our own house.

EDDIE: You're welcome, Marco, we got plenty of room here. Katie, give them supper, heh? *Exits into bedroom with their bags.*

CATHERINE: Come here, sit down. I'll get you some soup.

MARCO, *as they go to the table:* We ate on the ship. Thank you. *To Eddie, calling off to bedroom:* Thank you.

BEATRICE: Get some coffee. We'll all have coffee. Come sit down.
Rodolpho and Marco sit, at the table.

CATHERINE, *wondrously:* How come he's so dark and you're so light, Rodolpho?

RODOLPHO, *ready to laugh:* I don't know. A thousand years ago, they say, the Danes invaded Sicily.

Beatrice kisses Rodolpho. They laugh as Eddie enters.

CATHERINE, *to Beatrice:* He's practically blond!

EDDIE: How's the coffee doin'?

CATHERINE, *brought up:* I'm gettin' it. *She hurries out to kitchen.*

EDDIE *sits on his rocker:* Yiz have a nice trip?

MARCO: The ocean is always rough. But we are good sailors.

EDDIE: No trouble gettin' here?

MARCO: No. The man brought us. Very nice man.

RODOLPHO, *to Eddie:* He says we start to work tomorrow. Is he honest?

EDDIE, *laughing:* No. But as long as you owe them money, they'll get you plenty of work. *To Marco:* Yiz ever work on the piers in Italy?

MARCO: Piers? Ts!—no.

RODOLPHO, *smiling at the smallness of his town:* In our town there are no piers, only the beach, and little fishing boats.

BEATRICE: So what kinda work did yiz do?

MARCO, *shrugging shyly, even embarrassed:* Whatever there is, anything.

RODOLPHO: Sometimes they build a house, or if they fix the bridge —Marco is a mason and I bring him the cement. *He laughs.* In harvest time we work in the fields . . . if there is work. Anything.

EDDIE: Still bad there, heh?

MARCO: Bad, yes.

RODOLPHO, *laughing:* It's terrible! We stand around all day in the piazza listening to the fountain like birds. Everybody waits only for the train.

BEATRICE: What's on the train?

RODOLPHO: Nothing. But if there are many passengers and you're lucky you make a few lire to push the taxi up the hill.

Enter Catherine; she listens.

BEATRICE: You gotta push a taxi?

RODOLPHO, *laughing:* Oh, sure! It's a feature in our town. The horses in our town are skinnier than goats. So if there are too many passengers we help to push the carriages up to the hotel. *He laughs.* In our town the horses are only for show.

CATHERINE: Why don't they have automobile taxis?

RODOLPHO: There is one. We push that too. *They laugh.* Everything in our town, you gotta push!

BEATRICE, *to Eddie:* How do you like that!

EDDIE, *to Marco:* So what're you wanna do, you gonna stay here in this country or you wanna go back?

MARCO, *surprised:* Go back?

EDDIE: Well, you're married, ain't you?

MARCO: Yes. I havè three children.

BEATRICE: Three! I thought only one.

MARCO: Oh, no. I have three now. Four years, five years, six years.

BEATRICE: Ah . . . I bet they're cryin' for you already, heh?

MARCO: What can I do? The older one is sick in his chest. My wife—she feeds them from her own mouth. I tell you the truth, if I stay there they will never grow up. They eat the sunshine.

BEATRICE: My God. So how long you want to stay?

MARCO: With your permission, we will stay maybe a—

EDDIE: She don't mean in this house, she means in the country.

MARCO: Oh. Maybe four, five, six years, I think.

RODOLPHO, *smiling:* He trusts his wife.

BEATRICE: Yeah, but maybe you'll get enough, you'll be able to go back quicker.

MARCO: I hope. I don't know. *To Eddie:* I understand it's not so good here either.

EDDIE: Oh, you guys'll be all right—till you pay them off, anyway. After that, you'll have to scramble, that's all. But you'll make better here than you could there.

RODOLPHO: How much? We hear all kinds of figures. How much can a man make? We work hard, we'll work all day, all night—

    Marco raises a hand to hush him.

EDDIE—*he is coming more and more to address Marco only:* On the average a whole year? Maybe—well, it's hard to say, see. Sometimes we lay off, there's no ships three four weeks.

MARCO: Three, four weeks!—Ts!

EDDIE: But I think you could probably—thirty, forty a week, over the whole twelve months of the year.

MARCO, *rises, crosses to Eddie:* Dollars.

EDDIE: Sure dollars.

Marco puts an arm round Rodolpho and they laugh.

MARCO: If we can stay here a few months, Beatrice—

BEATRICE: Listen, you're welcome, Marco—

MARCO: Because I could send them a little more if I stay here.

BEATRICE: As long as you want, we got plenty a room.

MARCO, *his eyes are showing tears:* My wife— *To Eddie:* My wife —I want to send right away maybe twenty dollars—

EDDIE: You could send them something next week already.

MARCO—*he is near tears:* Eduardo . . . *He goes to Eddie, offering his hand.*

EDDIE: Don't thank me. Listen, what the hell, it's no skin off me. *To Catherine:* What happened to the coffee?

CATHERINE: I got it on. *To Rodolpho:* You married too? No.

RODOLPHO *rises:* Oh, no . . .

BEATRICE, *to Catherine:* I told you he—

CATHERINE: I know, I just thought maybe he got married recently.

RODOLPHO: I have no money to get married. I have a nice face, but no money. *He laughs.*

CATHERINE, *to Beatrice:* He's a real blond!

BEATRICE, *to Rodolpho:* You want to stay here too, heh? For good?

RODOLPHO: Me? Yes, forever! Me, I want to be an American. And then I want to go back to Italy when I am rich, and I will buy a motorcycle. *He smiles. Marco shakes him affectionately.*

CATHERINE: A motorcycle!

RODOLPHO: With a motorcycle in Italy you will never starve any more.

BEATRICE: I'll get you coffee. *She exits to the kitchen.*

EDDIE: What you do with a motorcycle?

MARCO: He dreams, he dreams.

RODOLPHO, *to Marco:* Why? *To Eddie:* Messages! The rich people in the hotel always need someone who will carry a message. But quickly, and with a great noise. With a blue motorcycle I would station myself in the courtyard of the hotel, and in a little while I would have messages.

MARCO: When you have no wife you have dreams.

EDDIE: Why can't you just walk, or take a trolley or sump'm?

Enter Beatrice with coffee.

RODOLPHO: Oh, no, the machine, the machine is necessary. A man comes into a great hotel and says, I am a messenger. Who is this man? He disappears walking, there is no noise, nothing. Maybe he will never come back, maybe he will never deliver the message. But a man who rides up on a great machine, this man is responsible, this man exists. He will be given messages. *He helps Beatrice set out the coffee things.* I am also a singer, though.

EDDIE: You mean a regular—?

RODOLPHO: Oh, yes. One night last year Andreola got sick. Baritone. And I took his place in the garden of the hotel. Three arias I sang without a mistake! Thousand-lire notes they threw from the tables, money was falling like a storm in the treasury. It was magnificent. We lived six months on that night, eh, Marco?

Marco nods doubtfully.

MARCO: Two months.

Eddie laughs.

BEATRICE: Can't you get a job in that place?

RODOLPHO: Andreola got better. He's a baritone, very strong.

Beatrice laughs.

MARCO, *regretfully, to Beatrice:* He sang too loud.

RODOLPHO: Why too loud?

MARCO: Too loud. The guests in that hotel are all Englishmen. They don't like too loud.

RODOLPHO, *to Catherine:* Nobody ever said it was too loud!

MARCO: I say. It was too loud. *To Beatrice:* I knew it as soon as he started to sing. Too loud.

RODOLPHO: Then why did they throw so much money?

MARCO: They paid for your courage. The English like courage. But once is enough.

RODOLPHO, *to all but Marco:* I never heard anybody say it was too loud.

CATHERINE: Did you ever hear of jazz?

RODOLPHO: Oh, sure! I *sing* jazz.

CATHERINE *rises:* You could sing jazz?

RODOLPHO: Oh, I sing Napolidan, jazz, bel canto— I sing "Paper Doll," you like "Paper Doll"?

CATHERINE: Oh, sure, I'm crazy for "Paper Doll." Go ahead, sing it.

RODOLPHO *takes his stance after getting a nod of permission from Marco, and with a high tenor voice begins singing:*

"I'll tell you boys it's tough to be alone,
 And it's tough to love a doll that's not your own.
 I'm through with all of them,
 I'll never fall again,
 Hey, boy, what you gonna do?
 I'm gonna buy a paper doll that I can call my own,
 A doll that other fellows cannot steal.

Eddie rises and moves upstage.

 And then those flirty, flirty guys
 With their flirty, flirty eyes
 Will have to flirt with dollies that are real—

EDDIE: Hey, kid—hey, wait a minute—

CATHERINE, *enthralled:* Leave him finish, it's beautiful! *To Beatrice:* He's terrific! It's terrific, Rodolpho.

EDDIE: Look, kid; you don't want to be picked up, do ya?

MARCO: No—no! *He rises.*

EDDIE, *indicating the rest of the building:* Because we never had no singers here . . . and all of a sudden there's a singer in the house, y'know what I mean?

MARCO: Yes, yes. You'll be quiet, Rodolpho.

EDDIE—*he is flushed:* They got guys all over the place, Marco. I mean.

MARCO: Yes. He'll be quiet. *To Rodolpho:* You'll be quiet.

Rodolpho nods.

Eddie has risen, with iron control, even a smile. He moves to Catherine.

EDDIE: What's the high heels for, Garbo?

CATHERINE: I figured for tonight—

EDDIE: Do me a favor, will you? Go ahead.

Embarrassed now, angered, Catherine goes out into the bedroom. Beatrice watches her go and gets up; in passing, she gives

*Eddie a cold look, restrained only by the strangers, and goes to
the table to pour coffee.*

EDDIE, *striving to laugh, and to Marco, but directed as much to
Beatrice:* All actresses they want to be around here.

RODOLPHO, *happy about it:* In Italy too! All the girls.

   *Catherine emerges from the bedroom in low-heel shoes,
comes to the table. Rodolpho is lifting a cup.*

EDDIE—*he is sizing up Rodolpho, and there is a concealed sus-
picion:* Yeah, heh?

RODOLPHO: Yes! *Laughs, indicating Catherine:* Especially when
they are so beautiful!

CATHERINE: You like sugar?

RODOLPHO: Sugar? Yes! I like sugar very much!

   *Eddie is downstage, watching as she pours a spoonful of sugar
into his cup, his face puffed with trouble, and the room dies.*

   Lights rise on Alfieri.

ALFIERI: Who can ever know what will be discovered? Eddie
Carbone had never expected to have a destiny. A man works,
raises his family, goes bowling, eats, gets old, and then he dies.
Now, as the weeks passed, there was a future, there was a trouble
that would not go away.

   *The lights fade on Alfieri, then rise on Eddie standing at the
doorway of the house. Beatrice enters on the street. She sees Eddie,
smiles at him. He looks away.*

   She starts to enter the house when Eddie speaks.

EDDIE: It's after eight.

BEATRICE: Well, it's a long show at the Paramount.

EDDIE: They must've seen every picture in Brooklyn by now. He's
supposed to stay in the house when he ain't working. He ain't
supposed to go advertising himself.

BEATRICE: Well that's his trouble, what do you care? If they pick
him up they pick him up, that's all. Come in the house.

EDDIE: What happened to the stenography? I don't see her practice no more.

BEATRICE: She'll get back to it. She's excited, Eddie.

EDDIE: She tell you anything?

BEATRICE *comes to him, now the subject is opened:* What's the
matter with you? He's a nice kid, what do you want from him?

EDDIE: That's a nice kid? He gives me the heeby-jeebies.

BEATRICE, *smiling:* Ah, go on, you're just jealous.

EDDIE: Of *him?* Boy, you don't think much of me.

BEATRICE: I don't understand you. What's so terrible about him?

EDDIE: You mean it's all right with you? That's gonna be her husband?

BEATRICE: Why? He's a nice fella, hard workin', he's a good-lookin' fella.

EDDIE: He sings on the ships, didja know that?

BEATRICE: What do you mean, he sings?

EDDIE: Just what I said, he sings. Right on the deck, all of a sudden, a whole song comes out of his mouth—with motions. You know what they're callin' him now? Paper Doll they're callin' him, Canary. He's like a weird. He comes out on the pier, one-two-three, it's a regular free show.

BEATRICE: Well, he's a kid; he don't know how to behave himself yet.

EDDIE: And with that wacky hair; he's like a chorus girl or sump'm.

BEATRICE: So he's blond, so—

EDDIE: I just hope that's his regular hair, that's all I hope.

BEATRICE: You crazy or sump'm? *She tries to turn him to her.*

EDDIE—*he keeps his head turned away:* What's so crazy? I don't like his whole way.

BEATRICE: Listen, you never seen a blond guy in your life? What about Whitey Balso?

EDDIE, *turning to her victoriously:* Sure, but Whitey don't sing; he don't do like that on the ships.

BEATRICE: Well, maybe that's the way they do in Italy.

EDDIE: Then why don't his brother sing? Marco goes around like a man; nobody kids Marco. *He moves from her, halts. She realizes there is a campaign solidified in him.* I tell you the truth I'm surprised I have to tell you all this. I mean I'm surprised, B.

BEATRICE—*she goes to him with purpose now:* Listen, you ain't gonna start nothin' here.

EDDIE: I ain't startin' nothin', but I ain't gonna stand around lookin' at that. For that character I didn't bring her up. I swear, B., I'm surprised at you; I sit there waitin' for you to wake up but everything is great with you.

BEATRICE: No, everything ain't great with me.

EDDIE: No?

BEATRICE: No. But I got other worries.

EDDIE: Yeah. *He is already weakening.*

BEATRICE: Yeah, you want me to tell you?

EDDIE, *in retreat:* Why? What worries you got?

BEATRICE: When am I gonna be a wife again, Eddie?

EDDIE: I ain't been feelin' good. They bother me since they came.

BEATRICE: It's almost three months you don't feel good; they're only here a couple of weeks. It's three months, Eddie.

EDDIE: I don't know, B. I don't want to talk about it.

BEATRICE: What's the matter, Eddie, you don't like me, heh?

EDDIE: What do you mean, I don't like you? I said I don't feel good, that's all.

BEATRICE: Well, tell me, am I doing something wrong? Talk to me.

EDDIE—*Pause. He can't speak, then:* I can't. I can't talk about it.

BEATRICE: Well tell me what—

EDDIE: I got nothin' to say about it!

She stands for a moment; he is looking off; she turns to go into the house.

EDDIE: I'll be all right, B.; just lay off me, will ya? I'm worried about her.

BEATRICE: The girl is gonna be eighteen years old, it's time already.

EDDIE: B., he's taking her for a ride!

BEATRICE: All right, that's her ride. What're you gonna stand over her till she's forty? Eddie, I want you to cut it out now, you hear me? I don't like it! Now come in the house.

EDDIE: I want to take a walk, I'll be in right away.

BEATRICE: They ain't goin' to come any quicker if you stand in the street. It ain't nice, Eddie.

EDDIE: I'll be in right away. Go ahead. *He walks off.*

She goes into the house. Eddie glances up the street, sees Louis and Mike coming, and sits on an iron railing. Louis and Mike enter.

LOUIS: Wanna go bowlin' tonight?

EDDIE: I'm too tired. Goin' to sleep.

LOUIS: How's your two submarines?

EDDIE: They're okay.

LOUIS: I see they're gettin' work allatime.

EDDIE: Oh yeah, they're doin' all right.

MIKE: That's what we oughta do. We oughta leave the country and come in under the water. Then we get work.

EDDIE: You ain't kiddin'.

LOUIS: Well, what the hell. Y'know?

EDDIE: Sure.

LOUIS—*sits on railing beside Eddie:* Believe me, Eddie, you got a lotta credit comin' to you.

EDDIE: Aah, they don't bother me, don't cost me nutt'n.

MIKE: That older one, boy, he's a regular bull. I seen him the other day liftin' coffee bags over the Matson Line. They leave him alone he woulda load the whole ship by himself.

EDDIE: Yeah, he's a strong guy, that guy. Their father was a regular giant, supposed to be.

LOUIS: Yeah, you could see. He's a regular slave.

MIKE, *grinning:* That blond one, though— *Eddie looks at him.* He's got a sense of humor. *Louis snickers.*

EDDIE, *searchingly:* Yeah. He's funny—

MIKE, *starting to laugh:* Well he ain't exackly funny, but he's always like makin' remarks like, y'know? He comes around, everybody's laughin'. *Louis laughs.*

EDDIE, *uncomfortably, grinning:* Yeah, well . . . he's got a sense of humor.

MIKE, *laughing:* Yeah, I mean, he's always makin' like remarks, like, y'know?

EDDIE: Yeah, I know. But he's a kid yet, y'know? He—he's just a kid, that's all.

MIKE, *getting hysterical with Louis:* I know. You take one look at him—everybody's happy. *Louis laughs.* I worked one day with him last week over the Moore-MacCormack Line, I'm tellin' you they was all hysterical. *Louis and he explode in laughter.*

EDDIE: Why? What'd he do?

MIKE: I don't know . . . he was just humorous. You never can remember what he says, y'know? But it's the way he says it. I mean he gives you a look sometimes and you start laughin'!

EDDIE: Yeah. *Troubled:* He's got a sense of humor.

MIKE, *gasping:* Yeah.

LOUIS, *rising:* Well, we see ya, Eddie.

EDDIE: Take it easy.

LOUIS: Yeah. See ya.

MIKE: If you wanna come bowlin' later we're goin' Flatbush Avenue.

Laughing, they move to exit, meeting Rodolpho and Catherine entering on the street. Their laughter rises as they see Rodolpho, who does not understand but joins in. Eddie moves to enter the house as Louis and Mike exit. Catherine stops him at the door.

CATHERINE: Hey, Eddie—what a picture we saw! Did we laugh!

EDDIE—*he can't help smiling at sight of her:* Where'd you go?

CATHERINE: Paramount. It was with those two guys, y'know? That—

EDDIE: Brooklyn Paramount?

CATHERINE, *with an edge of anger, embarrassed before Rodolpho:* Sure, the Brooklyn Paramount. I told you we wasn't goin' to New York.

EDDIE, *retreating before the threat of her anger:* All right, I only asked you. *To Rodolpho:* I just don't· want her hangin' around Times Square, see? It's full of tramps over there.

RODOLPHO: I would like to go to Broadway once, Eddie. I would like to walk with her once where the theaters are and the opera. Since I was a boy I see pictures of those lights.

EDDIE, *his little patience waning:* I want to talk to her a minute, Rodolpho. Go inside, will you?

RODOLPHO: Eddie, we only walk together in the streets. She teaches me.

CATHERINE: You know what he can't get over? That there's no fountains in Brooklyn!

EDDIE, *smiling unwillingly:* Fountains? *Rodolpho smiles at his own naïveté.*

CATHERINE: In Italy he says, every town's got fountains, and they meet there. And you know what? They got oranges on the trees where he comes from, and lemons. Imagine—on the trees? I mean it's interesting. But he's crazy for New York.

RODOLPHO, *attempting familiarity:* Eddie, why can't we go once to Broadway—?

EDDIE: Look, I gotta tell her something—

RODOLPHO: Maybe you can come too. I want to see all those

lights. *He sees no response in Eddie's face. He glances at Catherine.* I'll walk by the river before I go to sleep. *He walks off down the street.*

CATHERINE: Why don't you talk to him, Eddie? He blesses you, and you don't talk to him hardly.

EDDIE, *enveloping her with his eyes:* I bless you and you don't talk to me. *He tries to smile.*

CATHERINE: *I* don't talk to you? *She hits his arm.* What do you mean?

EDDIE: I don't see you no more. I come home you're runnin' around someplace—

CATHERINE: Well, he wants to see everything, that's all, so we go. . . . You mad at me?

EDDIE: No. *He moves from her, smiling sadly.* It's just I used to come home, you was always there. Now, I turn around, you're a big girl. I don't know how to talk to you.

CATHERINE: Why?

EDDIE: I don't know, you're runnin', you're runnin', Katie. I don't think you listening any more to me.

CATHERINE, *going to him:* Ah, Eddie, sure I am. What's the matter? You don't like him?

  Slight pause.

EDDIE, *turns to her:* You like him, Katie?

CATHERINE, *with a blush but holding her ground:* Yeah. I like him.

EDDIE—*his smile goes:* You like him.

CATHERINE, *looking down:* Yeah. *Now she looks at him for the consequences, smiling but tense. He looks at her like a lost boy.* What're you got against him? I don't understand. He only blesses you.

EDDIE *turns away:* He don't bless me, Katie.

CATHERINE: He does! You're like a father to him!

EDDIE *turns to her:* Katie.

CATHERINE: What, Eddie?

EDDIE: You gonna marry him?

CATHERINE: I don't know. We just been . . . goin' around, that's all. *Turns to him:* What're you got against him, Eddie? Please, tell me. What?

EDDIE: He don't respect you.

CATHERINE: Why?

EDDIE: Katie . . . if you wasn't an orphan, wouldn't he ask your father's permission before he run around with you like this?

CATHERINE: Oh, well, he didn't think you'd mind.

EDDIE: He knows I mind, but it don't bother him if I mind, don't you see that?

CATHERINE: No, Eddie, he's got all kinds of respect for me. And you too! We walk across the street he takes my arm—he almost bows to me! You got him all wrong, Eddie; I mean it, you—

EDDIE: Katie, he's only bowin' to his passport.

CATHERINE: His passport!

EDDIE: That's right. He marries you he's got the right to be an American citizen. That's what's goin' on here. *She is puzzled and surprised.* You understand what I'm tellin' you? The guy is lookin' for his break, that's all he's lookin' for.

CATHERINE, *pained:* Oh, no, Eddie, I don't think so.

EDDIE: You don't think so! Katie, you're gonna make me cry here. Is that a workin' man? What does he do with his first money? A snappy new jacket he buys, records, a pointy pair new shoes and his brother's kids are starvin' over there with tuberculosis? That's a hit-and-run guy, baby; he's got bright lights in his head, Broadway. Them guys don't think of nobody but theirself! You marry him and the next time you see him it'll be for divorce!

CATHERINE *steps toward him:* Eddie, he never said a word about his papers or—

EDDIE: You mean he's supposed to tell you that?

CATHERINE: I don't think he's even thinking about it.

EDDIE: What's better for him to think about! He could be picked up any day here and he's back pushin' taxis up the hill!

CATHERINE: No, I don't believe it.

EDDIE: Katie, don't break my heart, listen to me.

CATHERINE: I don't want to hear it.

EDDIE: Katie, listen . . .

CATHERINE: He loves me!

EDDIE, *with deep alarm:* Don't say that, for God's sake! This is the oldest racket in the country—

CATHERINE, *desperately, as though he had made his imprint:* I don't believe it! *She rushes to the house.*

EDDIE, *following her:* They been pullin' this since the Immigration Law was put in! They grab a green kid that don't know nothin' and they—

CATHERINE, *sobbing:* I don't believe it and I wish to hell you'd stop it!

EDDIE: Katie!

They enter the apartment. The lights in the living room have risen and Beatrice is there. She looks past the sobbing Catherine at Eddie, who in the presence of his wife, makes an awkward gesture of eroded command, indicating Catherine.

EDDIE: Why don't you straighten her out?

BEATRICE, *inwardly angered at his flowing emotion, which in itself alarms her:* When are you going to leave her alone?

EDDIE: B., the guy is no good!

BEATRICE, *suddenly, with open fright and fury:* You going to leave her alone? Or you gonna drive me crazy? *He turns, striving to retain his dignity, but nevertheless in guilt walks out of the house, into the street and away. Catherine starts into a bedroom.* Listen, Catherine. *Catherine halts, turns to her sheepishly.* What are you going to do with yourself?

CATHERINE: I don't know.

BEATRICE: Don't tell me you don't know; you're not a baby any more, what are you going to do with yourself?

CATHERINE: He won't listen to me.

BEATRICE: I don't understand this. He's not your father, Catherine. I don't understand what's going on here.

CATHERINE, *as one who herself is trying to rationalize a buried impulse:* What am I going to do, just kick him in the face with it?

BEATRICE: Look, honey, you wanna get married, or don't you wanna get married? What are you worried about, Katie?

CATHERINE, *quietly, trembling:* I don't know B. It just seems wrong if he's against it so much.

BEATRICE, *never losing her aroused alarm:* Sit down, honey, I want to tell you something. Here, sit down. Was there ever any fella he liked for you? There wasn't, was there?

CATHERINE: But he says Rodolpho's just after his papers.

BEATRICE: Look, he'll say anything. What does he care what he says? If it was a prince came here for you it would be no different. You know that, don't you?

CATHERINE: Yeah, I guess.

BEATRICE: So what does that mean?

CATHERINE *slowly turns her head to Beatrice:* What?

BEATRICE: It means you gotta be your own self more. You still think you're a little girl, honey. But nobody else can make up your mind for you any more, you understand? You gotta give him to understand that he can't give you orders no more.

CATHERINE: Yeah, but how am I going to do that? He thinks I'm a baby.

BEATRICE: Because *you* think you're a baby. I told you fifty times already, you can't act the way you act. You still walk around in front of him in your slip—

CATHERINE: Well I forgot.

BEATRICE: Well you can't do it. Or like you sit on the edge of the bathtub talkin' to him when he's shavin' in his underwear.

CATHERINE: When'd I do that?

BEATRICE: I seen you in there this morning.

CATHERINE: Oh . . . well, I wanted to tell him something and I—

BEATRICE: I know, honey. But if you act like a baby and he be treatin' you like a baby. Like when he comes home sometimes you throw yourself at him like when you was twelve years old.

CATHERINE: Well I like to see him and I'm happy so I—

BEATRICE: Look, I'm not tellin' you what to do honey, but—

CATHERINE: No, you could tell me, B.! Gee, I'm all mixed up. See, I— He looks so sad now and it hurts me.

BEATRICE: Well look Katie, if it's goin' to hurt you so much you're gonna end up an old maid here.

CATHERINE: No!

BEATRICE: I'm tellin' you, I'm not makin' a joke. I tried to tell you a couple of times in the last year or so. That's why I was so happy you were going to go out and get work, you wouldn't be here so much, you'd be a little more independent. I mean it. It's wonderful for a whole family to love each other, but you're a grown woman and you're in the same house with a grown man. So you'll act different now, heh?

CATHERINE: Yeah, I will. I'll remember.

BEATRICE: Because it ain't only up to him, Katie, you understand? I told him the same thing already.

CATHERINE, *quickly:* What?

BEATRICE: That he should let you go. But, you see, if only I tell him, he thinks I'm just bawlin' him out, or maybe I'm jealous or somethin', you know?

CATHERINE, *astonished:* He said you was jealous?

BEATRICE: No, I'm just sayin' maybe that's what he thinks. *She reaches over to Catherine's hand; with a strained smile:* You think I'm jealous of you, honey?

CATHERINE: No! It's the first I thought of it.

BEATRICE, *with a quiet sad laugh:* Well you should have thought of it before . . . but I'm not. We'll be all right. Just give him to understand; you don't have to fight, you're just— You're a woman, that's all, and you got a nice boy, and now the time came when you said good-by. All right?

CATHERINE, *strangely moved at the prospect:* All right. . . . If I can.

BEATRICE: Honey . . . you gotta.

Catherine, sensing now an imperious demand, turns with some fear, with a discovery, to Beatrice. She is at the edge of tears, as though a familiar world had shattered.

CATHERINE: Okay.

Lights out on them and up on Alfieri, seated behind his desk.

ALFIERI: It was at this time that he first came to me. I had represented his father in an accident case some years before, and I was acquainted with the family in a casual way. I remember him now as he walked through my doorway—

Enter Eddie down right ramp.

His eyes were like tunnels; my first thought was that he had committed a crime,

Eddie sits besides the desk, cap in hand, looking out.

but soon I saw it was only a passion that had moved into his body, like a stranger. *Alfieri pauses, looks down at his desk, then to Eddie as though he were continuing a conversation with him.* I don't quite understand what I can do for you. Is there a question of law somewhere?

EDDIE: That's what I want to ask you.

ALFIERI: Because there's nothing illegal about a girl falling in love with an immigrant.

EDDIE: Yeah, but what about it if the only reason for it is to get his papers?

ALFIERI: First of all you don't know that.

EDDIE: I see it in his eyes; he's laughin' at her and he's laughin' at me.

ALFIERI: Eddie, I'm a lawyer. I can only deal in what's provable. You understand that, don't you? Can you prove that?

EDDIE: *I know what's in his mind, Mr. Alfieri!*

ALFIERI: Eddie, even if you could prove that—

EDDIE: Listen . . . will you listen to me a minute? My father always said you was a smart man. I want you to listen to me.

ALFIERI: I'm only a lawyer, Eddie.

EDDIE: Will you listen a minute? I'm talkin' about the law. Lemme just bring out what I mean. A man, which he comes into the country illegal, don't it stand to reason he's gonna take every penny and put it in the sock? Because they don't know from one day to another, right?

ALFIERI: All right.

EDDIE: He's spendin'. Records he buys now. Shoes. Jackets. Y'understand me? This guy ain't worried. This guy is *here*. So it must be that he's got it all laid out in his mind already—he's stayin'. Right?

ALFIERI: Well? What about it?

EDDIE: All right. *He glances at Alfieri, then down to the floor.* I'm talking to you confidential, ain't I?

ALFIERI: Certainly.

EDDIE: I mean it don't go no place but here. Because I don't like to say this about anybody. Even my wife I didn't exactly say this.

ALFIERI: What is it?

EDDIE *takes a breath and glances briefly over each shoulder:* The guy ain't right, Mr. Alfieri.

ALFIERI: What do you mean?

EDDIE: I mean he ain't right.

ALFIERI: I don't get you.

EDDIE, *shifts to another position in the chair:* Dja ever get a look at him?

ALFIERI: Not that I know of, no.

EDDIE: He's a blond guy. Like . . . platinum. You know what I mean?

ALFIERI: No.

EDDIE: I mean if you close the paper fast—you could blow him over.

ALFIERI: Well that doesn't mean—

EDDIE: Wait a minute, I'm tellin' you sump'm. He sings, see. Which is—I mean it's all right, but sometimes he hits a note, see. I turn around. I mean—high. You know what I mean?

ALFIERI: Well, that's a tenor.

EDDIE: I know a tenor, Mr. Alfieri. This ain't no tenor. I mean if you came in the house and you didn't know who was singin', you wouldn't be lookin' for him you be lookin' for her.

ALFIERI: Yes, but that's not—

EDDIE: I'm tellin' you sump'm, wait a minute. Please, Mr. Alfieri. I'm tryin' to bring out my thoughts here. Couple of nights ago my niece brings out a dress which it's too small for her, because she shot up like a light this last year. He takes the dress, lays it on the table, he cuts it up; one-two-three, he makes a new dress. I mean he looked so sweet there, like an angel—you could kiss him he was so sweet.

ALFIERI: Now look, Eddie—

EDDIE: Mr. Alfieri, they're laughin' at him on the piers. I'm ashamed. Paper Doll they call him. Blondie now. His brother thinks it's because he's got a sense of humor, see—which he's got—but that ain't what they're laughin'. Which they're not goin' to come out with it because they know he's my relative, which they have to see me if they make a crack, y'know? But I know what they're laughin' at, and when I think of that guy layin' his hands on her I could—I mean it's eatin' me out, Mr. Alfieri, because I struggled for that girl. And now he comes in my house and—

ALFIERI: Eddie, look—I have my own children. I understand you. But the law is very specific. The law does not . . .

EDDIE, *with a fuller flow of indignation:* You mean to tell me that there's no law that a guy which he ain't right can go to work and marry a girl and—?

ALFIERI: You have no recourse in the law, Eddie.

EDDIE: Yeah, but if he ain't right, Mr. Alfieri, you mean to tell me—

ALFIERI: There is nothing you can do, Eddie, believe me.

EDDIE: Nothin'.

ALFIERI: Nothing at all. There's only one legal question here.

EDDIE: What?

ALFIERI: The manner in which they entered the country. But I don't think you want to do anything about that, do you?

EDDIE: You mean—?

ALFIERI: Well, they entered illegally.

EDDIE: Oh, Jesus, no, I wouldn't do nothin' about that, I mean—

ALFIERI: All right, then, let me talk now, eh?

EDDIE: Mr. Alfieri, I can't believe what you tell me. I mean there must be some kinda law which—

ALFIERI: Eddie, I want you to listen to me. *Pause.* You know, sometimes God mixes up the people. We all love somebody, the wife, the kids—every man's got somebody that he loves, heh? But sometimes . . . there's too much. You know? There's too much, and it goes where it mustn't. A man works hard, he brings up a child, sometimes it's a niece, sometimes even a daughter, and he never realizes it, but through the years—there is too much love for the daughter, there is too much love for the niece. Do you understand what I'm saying to you?

EDDIE, *sardonically:* What do you mean, I shouldn't look out for her good?

ALFIERI: Yes, but these things have to end, Eddie, that's all. The child has to grow up and go away, and the man has to learn to forget. Because after all, Eddie—what other way can it end? *Pause.* Let her go. That's my advice. You did your job, now it's her life; wish her luck, and let her go. *Pause.* Will you do that? Because there's no law, Eddie; make up your mind to it; the law is not interested in this.

EDDIE: You mean to tell me, even if he's a punk? If he's—

ALFIERI: There's nothing you can do.

Eddie stands.

EDDIE: Well, all right, thanks. Thanks very much.

ALFIERI: What are you going to do?

EDDIE, *with a helpless but ironic gesture:* What can I do? I'm a patsy, what can a patsy do? I worked like a dog twenty years so a punk could have her, so that's what I done. I mean, in the worst times, in the worst, when there wasn't a ship comin' in the harbor, I didn't stand around lookin' for relief—I hustled. When there was empty piers in Brooklyn I went to Hoboken, Staten

Island, the West Side, Jersey, all over—because I made a promise. I took out of my own mouth to give to her. I took out of my wife's mouth. I walked hungry plenty days in this city! *It begins to break through.* And now I gotta sit in my own house and look at a son-of-a-bitch punk like that—which he came out of nowhere! I give him my house to sleep! I take the blankets off my bed for him, and he takes and puts his dirty filthy hands on her like a goddam thief!

ALFIERI, *rising:* But, Eddie, she's a woman now.

EDDIE: He's stealing from me!

ALFIERI: She wants to get married, Eddie. She can't marry you, can she?

EDDIE, *furiously:* What're you talkin' about, marry me! I don't know what the hell you're talkin' about!

    Pause.

ALFIERI: I gave you my advice, Eddie. That's it.

    Eddie gathers himself. A pause.

EDDIE: Well, thanks. Thanks very much. It just—it's breakin' my heart, y'know. I—

ALFIERI: I understand. Put it out of your mind. Can you do that?

EDDIE: I'm— *He feels the threat of sobs, and with a helpless wave.* I'll see you around. *He goes out up the right ramp.*

ALFIERI *sits on desk:* There are times when you want to spread an alarm, but nothing has happened. I knew, I knew then and there— I could have finished the whole story that afternoon. It wasn't as though there was a mystery to unravel. I could see every step coming, step after step, like a dark figure walking down a hall toward a certain door. I knew where he was heading for, I knew where he was going to end. And I sat here many afternoons asking myself why, being an intelligent man, I was so powerless to stop it. I even went to a certain old lady in the neighborhood, a very wise old woman, and I told her, and she only nodded, and said, "Pray for him . . ." And so I—waited here.

    As lights go out on Alfieri, they rise in the apartment where all are finishing dinner. Beatrice and Catherine are clearing the table.

CATHERINE: You know where they went?

BEATRICE: Where?

CATHERINE: They went to Africa once. On a fishing boat. *Eddie glances at her.* It's true, Eddie.

Beatrice exits into the kitchen with dishes.

EDDIE: I didn't say nothin'. *He goes to his rocker, picks up a newspaper.*

CATHERINE: And I was never even in Staten Island.

EDDIE, *sitting with the paper:* You didn't miss nothin'. *Pause. Catherine takes dishes out.* How long that take you, Marco—to get to Africa?

MARCO, *rising:* Oh . . . two days. We go all over.

RODOLPHO, *rising:* Once we went to Yugoslavia.

EDDIE, *to Marco:* They pay all right on them boats?

Beatrice enters. She and Rodolpho stack the remaining dishes.

MARCO: If they catch fish they pay all right. *Sits on a stool.*

RODOLPHO: They're family boats, though. And nobody in our family owned one. So we only worked when one of the families was sick.

BEATRICE: Y'know, Marco, what I don't understand—there's an ocean full of fish and yiz are all starvin'.

EDDIE: They gotta have boats, nets, you need money.

Catherine enters.

BEATRICE: Yeah, but couldn't they like fish from the beach? You see them down Coney Island—

MARCO: Sardines.

EDDIE: Sure. *Laughing:* How you gonna catch sardines on a hook?

BEATRICE: Oh, I didn't know they're sardines. *To Catherine:* They're sardines!

CATHERINE: Yeah, they follow them all over the ocean, Africa, Yugoslavia . . . *She sits and begins to look through a movie magazine. Rodolpho joins her.*

BEATRICE, *to Eddie:* It's funny, y'know. You never think of it, that sardines are swimming in the ocean! *She exits to kitchen with dishes.*

CATHERINE: I know. It's like oranges and lemons on a tree. *To Eddie:* I mean you ever think of oranges and lemons on a tree?

EDDIE: Yeah, I know. It's funny. *To Marco:* I heard that they paint the oranges to make them look orange.

Beatrice enters.

MARCO—*He has been reading a letter:* Paint?

EDDIE: Yeah, I heard that they grow like green.

MARCO: No, in Italy the oranges are orange.

RODOLPHO: Lemons are green.

EDDIE, *resenting his instruction:* I know lemons are green, for Christ's sake, you see them in the store they're green sometimes. I said oranges they paint, I didn't say nothin' about lemons.

BEATRICE, *sitting; diverting their attention:* Your wife is gettin' the money all right, Marco?

MARCO: Oh, yes. She bought medicine for my boy.

BEATRICE: That's wonderful. You feel better, heh?

MARCO: Oh, yes! But I'm lonesome.

BEATRICE: I just hope you ain't gonna do like some of them around here. They're here twenty-five years, some men, and they didn't get enough together to go back twice.

MARCO: Oh, I know. We have many families in our town, the children never saw the father. But I will go home. Three, four years, I think.

BEATRICE: Maybe you should keep more here. Because maybe she thinks it comes so easy you'll never get ahead of yourself.

MARCO: Oh, no, she saves. I send everything. My wife is very lonesome. *He smiles shyly.*

BEATRICE: She must be nice. She pretty? I bet, heh?

MARCO, *blushing:* No, but she understand everything.

RODOLPHO: Oh, he's got a clever wife!

EDDIE: I betcha there's plenty surprises sometimes when those guys get back there, heh?

MARCO: Surprises?

EDDIE, *laughing:* I mean, you know—they count the kids and there's a couple extra than when they left?

MARCO: No—no . . . The women wait, Eddie. Most. Most. Very few surprises.

RODOLPHO: It's more strict in our town. *Eddie looks at him now.* It's not so free.

EDDIE *rises, paces up and down:* It ain't so free here either, Rodolpho, like you think. I seen greenhorns sometimes get in trouble that way—they think just because a girl don't go around with a shawl over her head that she ain't strict, y'know? Girl don't have to wear black dress to be strict. Know what I mean?

RODOLPHO: Well, I always have respect—

EDDIE: I know, but in your town you wouldn't just drag off some girl without permission, I mean. *He turns.* You know what I mean, Marco? It ain't that much different here.

MARCO, *cautiously:* Yes.

BEATRICE: Well, he didn't exactly drag her off though, Eddie.

EDDIE: I know, but I seen some of them get the wrong idea sometimes. *To Rodolpho:* I mean it might be a little more free here but it's just as strict.

RODOLPHO: I have respect for her, Eddie. I do anything wrong?

EDDIE: Look, kid, I ain't her father, I'm only her uncle—

BEATRICE: Well then, be an uncle then. *Eddie looks at her, aware of her criticizing force.* I mean.

MARCO: No, Beatrice, if he does wrong you must tell him. *To Eddie:* What does he do wrong?

EDDIE: Well, Marco, till he came here she was never out on the street twelve o'clock at night.

MARCO, *to Rodolpho:* You come home early now.

BEATRICE, *to Catherine:* Well, you said the movie ended late, didn't you?

CATHERINE: Yeah.

BEATRICE: Well, tell him, honey. *To Eddie:* The movie ended late.

EDDIE: Look, B., I'm just sayin'—he thinks she always stayed out like that.

MARCO: You come home early now, Rodolpho.

RODOLPHO, *embarrassed:* All right, sure. But I can't stay in the house all the time, Eddie.

EDDIE: Look, kid, I'm not only talkin' about her. The more you run around like that the more chance you're takin'. *To Beatrice:* I mean suppose he gets hit by a car or something. *To Marco:* Where's his papers, who is he? Know what I mean?

BEATRICE: Yeah, but who is he in the daytime, though? It's the same chance in the daytime.

EDDIE, *holding back a voice full of anger:* Yeah, but he don't have to go lookin' for it, Beatrice. If he's here to work, then he should work; if he's here for a good time then he could fool around! *To Marco:* But I understood, Marco, that you was both comin' to make a livin' for your family. You understand me, don't you, Marco? *He goes to his rocker.*

MARCO: I beg your pardon, Eddie.

EDDIE: I mean, that's what I understood in the first place, see.

MARCO: Yes. That's why we came.

EDDIE *sits on his rocker:* Well, that's all I'm askin'.

> *Eddie reads his paper. There is a pause, an awkwardness. Now Catherine gets up and puts a record on the phonograph— "Paper Doll."*

CATHERINE, *flushed with revolt:* You wanna dance, Rodolpho?
> *Eddie freezes.*

RODOLPHO, *in deference to Eddie:* No, I—I'm tired.

BEATRICE: Go ahead, dance, Rodolpho.

CATHERINE: Ah, come on. They got a beautiful quartet, these guys. Come.

> *She has taken his hand and he stiffly rises, feeling Eddie's eyes on his back, and they dance.*

EDDIE, *to Catherine:* What's that, a new record?

CATHERINE: It's the same one. We bought it the other day.

BEATRICE, *to Eddie:* They only bought three records. *She watches them dance; Eddie turns his head away. Marco just sits there, waiting. Now Beatrice turns to Eddie.* Must be nice to go all over in one of them fishin' boats. I would like that myself. See all them other countries?

EDDIE: Yeah.

BEATRICE, *to Marco:* But the women don't go along, I bet.

MARCO: No, not on the boats. Hard work.

BEATRICE: What're you got, a regular kitchen and everything?

MARCO: Yes, we eat very good on the boats—especially when Rodolpho comes along; everybody gets fat.

BEATRICE: Oh, he cooks?

MARCO: Sure, very good cook. Rice, pasta, fish, everything.

> *Eddie lowers his paper.*

EDDIE: He's a cook, too! *Looking at Rodolpho:* He sings, he cooks . . .

> *Rodolpho smiles thankfully.*

BEATRICE: Well it's good, he could always make a living.

EDDIE: It's wonderful. He sings, he cooks, he could make dresses . . .

CATHERINE: They get some high pay, them guys. The head chefs in all the big hotels are men. You read about them.

EDDIE: That's what I'm sayin'.

    Catherine and Rodolpho continue dancing.

CATHERINE: Yeah, well, I mean.

EDDIE, *to Beatrice:* He's lucky, believe me. *Slight pause. He looks away, then back to Beatrice.* That's why the water front is no place for him. *They stop dancing. Rodolpho turns off phonograph.* I mean like me—I can't cook, I can't sing, I can't make dresses, so I'm on the water front. But if I could cook, if I could sing, if I could make dresses, I wouldn't be on the water front. *He has been unconsciously twisting the newspaper into a tight roll. They are all regarding him now; he senses he is exposing the issue and he is driven on.* I would be someplace else. I would be like in a dress store. *He has bent the rolled paper and it suddenly tears in two. He suddenly gets up and pulls his pants up over his belly and goes to Marco.* What do you, say, Marco, we go to the bouts next Saturday night. You never seen a fight, did you?

MARCO, *uneasily:* Only in the moving pictures.

EDDIE, *going to Rodolpho:* I'll treat yiz. What do you say, Danish? You wanna come along? I'll buy the tickets.

RODOLPHO: Sure. I like to go.

CATHERINE *goes to Eddie; nervously happy now:* I'll make some coffee, all right?

EDDIE: Go ahead, make some! Make it nice and strong. *Mystified, she smiles and exits to kitchen. He is weirdly elated, rubbing his fists into his palms. He strides to Marco.* You wait, Marco, you see some real fights here. You ever do any boxing?

MARCO: No, I never.

EDDIE, *to Rodolpho:* Betcha you have done some, heh?

RODOLPHO: No.

EDDIE: Well, come on, I'll teach you.

BEATRICE: What's he got to learn that for?

EDDIE: Ya can't tell, one a these days somebody's liable to step on his foot or sump'm. Come on, Rodolpho, I show you a couple a passes. *He stands below table.*

BEATRICE: Go ahead, Rodolpho. He's a good boxer, he could teach you.

RODOLPHO, *embarrassed:* Well, I don't know how to— *He moves down to Eddie.*

EDDIE: Just put your hands up. Like this, see? That's right. That's very good, keep your left up, because you lead with the left, see, like this. *He gently moves his left into Rodolpho's face.* See? Now what you gotta do is you gotta block me, so when I come in like that you—*Rodolpho parries his left.* Hey, that's very good! *Rodolpho laughs.* All right, now come into me. Come on.

RODOLPHO: I don't want to hit you, Eddie.

EDDIE: Don't pity me, come on. Throw it, I'll show you how to block it. *Rodolpho jabs at him, laughing. The others join.* 'At's it. Come on again. For the jaw right here. *Rodolpho jabs with more assurance.* Very good!

BEATRICE, *to Marco:* He's very good!

Eddie crosses directly upstage of Rodolpho.

EDDIE: Sure, he's great! Come on, kid, put sump'm behind it, you can't hurt me. *Rodolpho, more seriously, jabs at Eddie's jaw and grazes it.* Attaboy.

Catherine comes from the kitchen, watches.

Now I'm gonna hit you, so block me, see?

CATHERINE, *with beginning alarm:* What are they doin'?

They are lightly boxing now.

BEATRICE—*she senses only the comradeship in it now:* He's teachin' him; he's very good!

EDDIE: Sure, he's terrific! Look at him go! *Rodolpho lands a blow.* 'At's it! Now, watch out, here I come, Danish! *He feints with his left hand and lands with his right. It mildly staggers Rodolpho. Marco rises.*

CATHERINE, *rushing to Rodolpho:* Eddie!

EDDIE: Why? I didn't hurt him. Did I hurt you, kid? *He rubs the back of his hand across his mouth.*

RODOLPHO: No, no, he didn't hurt me. *To Eddie with a certain gleam and a smile:* I was only surprised.

BEATRICE, *pulling Eddie down into the rocker:* That's enough, Eddie; he did pretty good though.

EDDIE: Yeah. *Rubbing his fists together:* He could be very good, Marco. I'll teach him again.

Marco nods at him dubiously.

RODOLPHO: Dance, Catherine. Come. *He takes her hand; they go to phonograph and start it. It plays "Paper Doll."*

Rodolpho takes her in his arms. They dance. Eddie in thought sits in his chair, and Marco takes a chair, places it in front of Eddie, and looks down at it. Beatrice and Eddie watch him.

MARCO: Can you lift this chair?

EDDIE: What do you mean?

MARCO: From here. *He gets on one knee with one hand behind his back, and grasps the bottom of one of the chair legs but does not raise it.*

EDDIE: Sure, why not? *He comes to the chair, kneels, grasps the leg, raises the chair one inch, but it leans over to the floor. Gee, that's hard, I never knew that. He tries again, and again fails. It's on an angle, that's why, heh?*

MARCO: Here. *He kneels, grasps, and with strain slowly raises the chair higher and higher, getting to his feet now. Rodolpho and Catherine have stopped dancing as Marco raises the chair over his head.*

Marco is face to face with Eddie, a strained tension gripping his eyes and jaw, his neck stiff, the chair raised like a weapon over Eddie's head—and he transforms what might appear like a glare of warning into a smile of triumph, and Eddie's grin vanishes as he absorbs his look.

CURTAIN

ACT TWO

Light rises on Alfieri at his desk.

ALFIERI: On the twenty-third of that December a case of Scotch whisky slipped from a net while being unloaded—as a case of Scotch whisky is inclined to do on the twenty-third of December on Pier Forty-one. There was no snow, but it was cold, his wife was out shopping. Marco was still at work. The boy had not been hired that day; Catherine told me later that this was the first time they had been alone together in the house.

Light is rising on Catherine in the apartment. Rodolpho is watching as she arranges a paper pattern on cloth spread on the table.

CATHERINE: You hungry?

RODOLPHO: Not for anything to eat. *Pause.* I have nearly three hundred dollars. Catherine?

CATHERINE: I heard you.

RODOLPHO: You don't like to talk about it any more?

CATHERINE: Sure, I don't mind talkin' about it.

RODOLPHO: What worries you, Catherine?

CATHERINE: I been wantin' to ask you about something. Could I?

RODOLPHO: All the answers are in my eyes, Catherine. But you don't look in my eyes lately. You're full of secrets. *She looks at him. She seems withdrawn.* What is the question?

CATHERINE: Suppose I wanted to live in Italy.

RODOLPHO, *smiling at the incongruity:* You going to marry somebody rich?

CATHERINE: No, I mean live there—you and me.

RODOLPHO, *his smile vanishing:* When?

CATHERINE: Well . . . when we get married.

RODOLPHO, *astonished:* You want to be an Italian?

CATHERINE: No, but I could live there without being Italian. Americans live there.

RODOLPHO: Forever?

CATHERINE: Yeah.

RODOLPHO *crosses to rocker:* You're fooling.

CATHERINE: No, I mean it.

RODOLPHO: Where do you get such an idea?

CATHERINE: Well, you're always saying it's so beautiful there, with the mountains and the ocean and all the—

RODOLPHO: You're fooling me.

CATHERINE: I mean it.

RODOLPHO *goes to her slowly:* Catherine, if I ever brought you home with no money, no business, nothing, they would call the priest and the doctor and they would say Rodolpho is crazy.

CATHERINE: I know, but I think we would be happier there.

RODOLPHO: Happier! What would you eat? You can't cook the view!

CATHERINE: Maybe you could be a singer, like in Rome or—

RODOLPHO: Rome! Rome is full of singers.

CATHERINE: Well, I could work then.

RODOLPHO: Where?

CATHERINE: God, there must be jobs somewhere!

RODOLPHO: There's nothing! Nothing, nothing, nothing. Now tell me what you're talking about. How can I bring you from a rich country to suffer in a poor country? What are you talking about? *She searches for words.* I would be a criminal stealing your face. In two years you would have an old, hungry face. When my brother's babies cry they give them water, water that boiled a bone. Don't you believe that?

CATHERINE, *quietly:* I'm afraid of Eddie here.

Slight pause.

RODOLPHO *steps closer to her:* We wouldn't live here. Once I am a citizen I could work anywhere and I would find better jobs and we would have a house, Catherine. If I were not afraid to be arrested I would start to be something wonderful here!

CATHERINE, *steeling herself:* Tell me something. I mean just tell me, Rodolpho—would you still want to do it if it turned out we had to go live in Italy? I mean just if it turned out that way.

RODOLPHO: This is your question or his question?

CATHERINE: I would like to know, Rodolpho. I mean it.

RODOLPHO: To go there with nothing.

CATHERINE: Yeah.

RODOLPHO: No. *She looks at him wide-eyed.* No.

CATHERINE: You wouldn't?

RODOLPHO: No; I will not marry you to live in Italy. I want you to be my wife, and I want to be a citizen. Tell him that, or I will. Yes. *He moves about angrily.* And tell him also, and tell yourself, please, that I am not a beggar, and you are not a horse, a gift, a favor for a poor immigrant.

CATHERINE: Well, don't get mad!

RODOLPHO: I am furious! *Goes to her.* Do you think I am so desperate? My brother is desperate, not me. You think I would carry on my back the rest of my life a woman I didn't love just to be an American? It's so wonderful? You think we have no tall buildings in Italy? Electric lights? No wide streets? No flags? No automobiles? Only work we don't have. I want to be an American so I can work, that is the only wonder here—work! How can you insult me, Catherine?

CATHERINE: I didn't mean that—

RODOLPHO: My heart dies to look at you. Why are you so afraid of him?

CATHERINE, *near tears:* I don't know!

RODOLPHO: Do you trust me, Catherine? You?

CATHERINE: It's only that I— He was good to me, Rodolpho. You don't know him; he was always the sweetest guy to me. Good. He razzes me all the time but he don't mean it. I know. I would—just feel ashamed if I made him sad. 'Cause I always dreamt that when I got married he would be happy at the wedding, and laughin'—and now he's—mad all the time and nasty— *She is weeping.* Tell him you'd live in Italy—just tell him, and maybe he would start to trust you a little, see? Because I want him to be happy; I mean—I like him, Rodolpho—and I can't stand it!

RODOLPHO: Oh, Catherine—oh, little girl.

CATHERINE: I love you, Rodolpho, I love you.

RODOLPHO: Then why are you afraid? That he'll spank you?

CATHERINE: Don't, don't laugh at me! I've been here all my life. . . . Every day I saw him when he left in the morning and when he came home at night. You think it's so easy to turn around and say to a man he's nothin' to you no more?

RODOLPHO: I know, but—

CATHERINE: You don't know; nobody knows! I'm not a baby, I know a lot more than people think I know. Beatrice says to be a woman, but—

RODOLPHO: Yes.

CATHERINE: Then why don't she be a woman? If I was a wife I would make a man happy instead of goin' at him all the time. I can tell a block away when he's blue in his mind and just wants to talk to somebody quiet and nice. . . . I can tell when he's hungry or wants a beer before he even says anything. I know when his feet hurt him, I mean I *know* him and now I'm supposed to turn around and make a stranger out of him? I don't know why I have to do that, I mean.

RODOLPHO: Catherine. If I take in my hands a little bird. And she grows and wishes to fly. But I will not let her out of my hands because I love her so much, is that right for me to do? I don't say you must hate him; but anyway you must go, mustn't you? Catherine?

CATHERINE, *softly:* Hold me.

RODOLPHO, *clasping her to him:* Oh, my little girl.

CATHERINE: Teach me. *She is weeping.* I don't know anything, teach me, Rodolpho, hold me.

RODOLPHO: There's nobody here now. Come inside. Come. *He is leading her toward the bedrooms.* And don't cry any more.

   Light rises on the street. In a moment Eddie appears. He is unsteady, drunk. He mounts the stairs. He enters the apartment, looks around, takes out a bottle from one pocket, puts it on the table. Then another bottle from another pocket, and a third from an inside pocket. He sees the pattern and cloth, goes over to it and touches it, and turns toward upstage.

EDDIE: Beatrice? *He goes to the open kitchen door and looks in.* Beatrice? Beatrice?

   Catherine enters from bedroom; under his gaze she adjusts her dress.

CATHERINE: You got home early.

EDDIE: Knocked off for Christmas early. *Indicating the pattern:* Rodolpho makin' you a dress?

CATHERINE: No. I'm makin' a blouse.

Rodolpho appears in the bedroom doorway. Eddie sees him and his arm jerks slightly in shock. Rodolpho nods to him testingly.

RODOLPHO: Beatrice went to buy presents for her mother.

Pause.

EDDIE: Pack it up. Go ahead. Get your stuff and get outa here. *Catherine instantly turns and walks toward the bedroom, and Eddie grabs her arm.* Where you goin'?

CATHERINE, *trembling with fright:* I think I have to get out of here, Eddie.

EDDIE: No, you ain't goin' nowheres, he's the one.

CATHERINE: I think I can't stay here no more. *She frees her arm, steps back toward the bedroom.* I'm sorry, Eddie. *She sees the tears in his eyes.* Well, don't cry. I'll be around the neighborhood; I'll see you. I just can't stay here no more. You know I can't. *Her sobs of pity and love for him break her composure.* Don't you know I can't? You know that, don't you? *She goes to him.* Wish me luck. *She clasps her hands prayerfully.* Oh, Eddie, don't be like that!

EDDIE: You ain't goin' nowheres.

CATHERINE: Eddie, I'm not gonna be a baby any more! You—

He reaches out suddenly, draws her to him, and as she strives to free herself he kisses her on the mouth.

RODOLPHO: Don't! *He pulls on Eddie's arm.* Stop that! Have respect for her!

EDDIE, *spun round by Rodolpho:* You want something?

RODOLPHO: Yes! She'll be my wife. That is what I want. My wife!

EDDIE: But what're you gonna be?

RODOLPHO: I show you what I be!

CATHERINE: Wait outside; don't argue with him!

EDDIE: Come on, show me! What're you gonna be? Show me!

RODOLPHO, *with tears of rage:* Don't say that to me!

Rodolpho flies at him in attack. Eddie pins his arms, laughing, and suddenly kisses him.

CATHERINE: Eddie! Let go, ya hear me! I'll kill you! Leggo of him!

She tears at Eddie's face and Eddie releases Rodolpho. Eddie

stands there with tears rolling down his face as he laughs mockingly at Rodolpho. She is staring at him in horror. Rodolpho is rigid. They are like animals that have torn at one another and broken up without a decision, each waiting for the other's mood.
EDDIE, *to Catherine:* You see? *To Rodolpho:* I give you till tomorrow, kid. Get outa here. Alone. You hear me? Alone.

CATHERINE: I'm going with him, Eddie. *She starts toward Rodolpho.*

EDDIE, *indicating Rodolpho with his head:* Not with that. *She halts, frightened. He sits, still panting for breath, and they watch him helplessly as he leans toward them over the table.* Don't make me do nuttin', Catherine. Watch your step, submarine. By rights they oughta throw you back in the water. But I got pity for you. *He moves unsteadily toward the door, always facing Rodolpho.* Just get outa here and don't lay another hand on her unless you wanna go out feet first. *He goes out of the apartment.*

   The lights go down, as they rise on Alfieri.

ALFIERI: On December twenty-seventh I saw him next. I normally go home well before six, but that day I sat around looking out my window at the bay, and when I saw him walking through my doorway, I knew why I had waited. And if I seem to tell this like a dream, it was that way. Several moments arrived in the course of the two talks we had when it occurred to me how—almost transfixed I had come to feel. I had lost my strength somewhere. *Eddie enters, removing his cap, sits in the chair, looks thoughtfully out.* I looked in his eyes more than I listened—in fact, I can hardly remember the conversation. But I will never forget how dark the room became when he looked at me; his eyes were like tunnels. I kept wanting to call the police, but nothing had happened. Nothing at all had really happened. *He breaks off and looks down at the desk. Then he turns to Eddie.* So in other words, he won't leave?

EDDIE: My wife is talkin' about renting a room upstairs for them. An old lady on the top floor is got an empty room.

ALFIERI: What does Marco say?

EDDIE: He just sits there. Marco don't say much.

ALFIERI: I guess they didn't tell him, heh? What happened?

EDDIE: I don't know; Marco don't say much.

ALFIERI: What does your wife say?

EDDIE, *unwilling to pursue this:* Nobody's talkin' much in the house. So what about that?

ALFIERI: But you didn't prove anything about him. It sounds like he just wasn't strong enough to break your grip.

EDDIE: I'm tellin' you I know—he ain't right. Somebody that don't want it can break it. Even a mouse, if you catch a teeny mouse and you hold it in your hand, that mouse can give you the right kind of fight. He didn't give me the right kind of fight, I know it, Mr. Alfieri, the guy ain't right.

ALFIERI: What did you do that for, Eddie?

EDDIE: To show her what he is! So she would see, once and for all! Her mother'll turn over in the grave! *He gathers himself almost peremptorily.* So what do I gotta do now? Tell me what to do.

ALFIERI: She actually said she's marrying him?

EDDIE: She told me, yeah. So what do I do?

    Slight pause.

ALFIERI: This is my last word, Eddie, take it or not, that's your business. Morally and legally you have no rights, you cannot stop it; she is a free agent.

EDDIE, *angering:* Didn't you hear what I told you?

ALFIERI, *with a tougher tone:* I heard what you told me, and I'm telling you what the answer is. I'm not only telling you now, I'm warning you—the law is nature. The law is only a word for what has a right to happen. When the law is wrong it's because it's unnatural, but in this case it is natural and a river will drown you if you buck it now. Let her go. And bless her. *A phone booth begins to glow on the opposite side of the stage; a faint, lonely blue. Eddie stands up, jaws clenched.* Somebody had to come for her, Eddie, sooner or later. *Eddie starts turning to go and Alfieri rises with new anxiety.* You won't have a friend in the world, Eddie! Even those who understand will turn against you, even the ones who feel the same will despise you! *Eddie moves off.* Put it out of your mind! Eddie! *He follows into the darkness, calling desperately.*

    Eddie is gone. The phone is glowing in light now. Light is out on Alfieri. Eddie has at the same time appeared beside the phone.

EDDIE: Give me the number of the Immigration Bureau. Thanks. *He dials.* I want to report something. Illegal immigrants. Two of them. That's right. Four-forty-one Saxon Street, Brooklyn, yeah. Ground floor. Heh? *With greater difficulty:* I'm just around the neighborhood, that's all. Heh?

Evidently he is being questioned further, and he slowly hangs up. He leaves the phone just as Louis and Mike come down the street.

LOUIS: Go bowlin', Eddie?

EDDIE: No, I'm due home.

LOUIS: Well, take it easy.

EDDIE: I'll see yiz.

They leave him, exiting right, and he watches them go. He glances about, then goes up into the house. The lights go on in the apartment. Beatrice is taking down Christmas decorations and packing them in a box.

EDDIE: Where is everybody? *Beatrice does not answer.* I says where is everybody?

BEATRICE, *looking up at him, wearied with it, and concealing a fear of him:* I decided to move them upstairs with Mrs. Dondero.

EDDIE: Oh, they're all moved up there already?

BEATRICE: Yeah.

EDDIE: Where's Catherine? She up there?

BEATRICE: Only to bring pillow cases.

EDDIE: She ain't movin' in with them.

BEATRICE: Look, I'm sick and tired of it. I'm sick and tired of it!

EDDIE: All right, all right, take it easy.

BEATRICE: I don't wanna hear no more about it, you understand? Nothin'!

EDDIE: What're you blowin' off about? Who brought them in here?

BEATRICE: All right, I'm sorry; I wish I'd a drop dead before I told them to come. In the ground I wish I was.

EDDIE: Don't drop dead, just keep in mind who brought them in here, that's all. *He moves about restlessly.* I mean I got a couple of rights here. *He moves, wanting to beat down her evident disapproval of him.* This is my house here not their house.

BEATRICE: What do you want from me? They're moved out; what do you want now?

EDDIE: I want my respect!

BEATRICE: So I moved them out, what more do you want? You got your house now, you got your respect.

EDDIE—*he moves about biting his lip:* I don't like the way you talk to me, Beatrice.

BEATRICE: I'm just tellin' you I done what you want!

EDDIE: I don't like it! The way you talk to me and the way you look at me. This is my house. And she is my niece and I'm responsible for her.

BEATRICE: So that's why you done that to him?

EDDIE: I done what to him?

BEATRICE: What you done to him in front of her; you know what I'm talkin' about. She goes around shakin' all the time, she can't go to sleep! That's what you call responsible for her?

EDDIE, *quietly:* The guy ain't right, Beatrice. *She is silent.* Did you hear what I said?

BEATRICE: Look, I'm finished with it. That's all. *She resumes her work.*

EDDIE, *helping her to pack the tinsel:* I'm gonna have it out with you one of these days, Beatrice.

BEATRICE: Nothin' to have out with me, it's all settled. Now we gonna be like it never happened, that's all.

EDDIE: I want my respect, Beatrice, and you know what I'm talkin' about.

BEATRICE: What?

Pause.

EDDIE—*finally his resolution hardens:* What I feel like doin' in the bed and what I don't feel like doin'. I don't want no—

BEATRICE: When'd I say anything about that?

EDDIE: You said, you said, I ain't deaf. I don't want no more conversations about that, Beatrice. I do what I feel like doin' or what I don't feel like doin'.

BEATRICE: Okay.

Pause.

EDDIE: You used to be different, Beatrice. You had a whole different way.

BEATRICE: *I'm* no different.

EDDIE: You didn't used to jump me all the time about everything. The last year or two I come in the house I don't know what's gonna hit me. It's a shootin' gallery in here and I'm the pigeon.

BEATRICE: Okay, okay.

EDDIE: Don't tell me okay, okay, I'm tellin' you the truth. A wife is supposed to believe the husband. If I tell you that guy ain't right don't tell me he is right.

BEATRICE: But how do you know?

EDDIE: Because I know. I don't go around makin' accusations. He give me the heeby-jeebies the first minute I seen him. And I don't like you sayin' I don't want her marryin' anybody. I broke my back payin' her stenography lessons so she could go out and meet a better class of people. Would I do that if I didn't want her to get married? Sometimes you talk like I was a crazy man or sump'm.

BEATRICE: But she likes him.

EDDIE: Beatrice, she's a baby, how is she gonna know what she likes?

BEATRICE: Well, you kept her a baby, you wouldn't let her go out. I told you a hundred times.

> *Pause.*

EDDIE: All right. Let her go out, then.

BEATRICE: She don't wanna go out now. It's too late, Eddie.

> *Pause.*

EDDIE: Suppose I told her to go out. Suppose I—

BEATRICE: They're going to get married next week, Eddie.

EDDIE—*his head jerks around to her:* She said that?

BEATRICE: Eddie, if you want my advice, go to her and tell her good luck. I think maybe now that you had it out you learned better.

EDDIE: What's the hurry next week?

BEATRICE: Well, she's been worried about him bein' picked up; this way he could start to be a citizen. She loves him, Eddie. *He gets up, moves about uneasily, restlessly.* Why don't you give her a good word? Because I still think she would like you to be a friend, y'know? *He is standing, looking at the floor.* I mean like if you told her you'd go to the wedding.

EDDIE: She asked you that?

BEATRICE: I know she would like it. I'd like to make a party here for her. I mean there oughta be some kinda send-off. Heh? I mean she'll have trouble enough in her life, let's start it off happy. What do you say? Cause in her heart she still loves you, Eddie. I know it. *He presses his fingers against his eyes.* What're you, cryin'? *She goes to him, holds his face.* Go . . . whyn't you go tell her you're sorry? *Catherine is seen on the upper landing of the stairway, and they hear her descending.* There . . . she's comin' down. Come on, shake hands with her.

EDDIE, *moving with suppressed suddenness:* No, I can't, I can't talk to her.

BEATRICE: Eddie, give her a break; a wedding should be happy!

EDDIE: I'm goin', I'm goin' for a walk.

He goes upstage for his jacket. Catherine enters and starts for the bedroom door.

BEATRICE: Katie? . . . Eddie, don't go, wait a minute. *She embraces Eddie's arm with warmth.* Ask him, Katie. Come on, honey.

EDDIE: It's all right, I'm— *He starts to go and she holds him.*

BEATRICE: No, she wants to ask you. Come on, Katie, ask him. We'll have a party! What're we gonna do, hate each other? Come on!

CATHERINE: I'm gonna get married, Eddie. So if you wanna come, the wedding be on Saturday.

Pause.

EDDIE: Okay. I only wanted the best for you, Katie. I hope you know that.

CATHERINE: Okay. *She starts out again.*

EDDIE: Catherine? *She turns to him.* I was just tellin' Beatrice . . . if you wanna go out, like . . . I mean I realize maybe I kept you home too much. Because he's the first guy you ever knew, y'know? I mean now that you got a job, you might meet some fellas, and you get a different idea, y'know? I mean you could always come back to him, you're still only kids, the both of yiz. What's the hurry? Maybe you'll get around a little bit, you grow up a little more, maybe you'll see different in a couple of months. I mean you be surprised, it don't have to be him.

CATHERINE: No, we made it up already.

EDDIE, *with increasing anxiety:* Katie, wait a minute.

CATHERINE: No, I made up my mind.

EDDIE: But you never knew no other fella, Katie! How could you make up your mind?

CATHERINE: Cause I did. I don't want nobody else.

EDDIE: But, Katie, suppose he gets picked up.

CATHERINE: That's why we gonna do it right away. Soon as we

finish the wedding he's goin' right over and start to be a citizen. I made up my mind, Eddie. I'm sorry. *To Beatrice:* Could I take two more pillow cases for the other guys?

BEATRICE: Sure, go ahead. Only don't let her forget where they came from.

Catherine goes into a bedroom.

EDDIE: She's got other boarders up there?

BEATRICE: Yeah, there's two guys that just came over.

EDDIE: What do you mean, came over?

BEATRICE: From Italy. Lipari the butcher—his nephew. They come from Bari, they just got here yesterday. I didn't even know till Marco and Rodolpho moved up there before. *Catherine enters, going toward exit with two pillow cases.* It'll be nice, they could all talk together.

EDDIE: Catherine! *She halts near the exit door. He takes in Beatrice too.* What're you, got no brains? You put them up there with two other submarines?

CATHERINE: Why?

EDDIE, *in a driving fright and anger:* Why! How do you know they're not trackin' these guys? They'll come up for them and find Marco and Rodolpho! Get them out of the house!

BEATRICE: But they been here so long already—

EDDIE: How do you know what enemies Lipari's got? Which they'd love to stab him in the back?

CATHERINE: Well what'll I do with them?

EDDIE: The neighborhood is full of rooms. Can't you stand to live a couple of blocks away from him? Get them out of the house!

CATHERINE: Well maybe tomorrow night I'll—

EDDIE: Not tomorrow, do it now. Catherine, you never mix yourself with somebody else's family! These guys get picked up, Lipari's liable to blame you or me and we got his whole family on our head. They got a temper, that family.

Two men in overcoats appear outside, start into the house.

CATHERINE: How'm I gonna find a place tonight?

EDDIE: Will you stop arguin' with me and get them out! You think I'm always tryin' to fool you or sump'm? What's the matter with you, don't you believe I could think of your good? Did I ever ask sump'm for myself? You think I got no feelin's? I never told you nothin' in my life that wasn't for your good. Nothin'!

And look at the way you talk to me! Like I was an enemy! Like I— *A knock on the door. His head swerves. They all stand motionless. Another knock. Eddie, in a whisper, pointing upstage.* Go up the fire escape, get them out over the back fence.

Catherine stands motionless, uncomprehending.

FIRST OFFICER, *in the hall:* Immigration! Open up in there!

EDDIE: Go, go. Hurry up! *She stands a moment staring at him in a realized horror.* Well, what're you lookin' at!

FIRST OFFICER: Open up!

EDDIE, *calling toward door:* Who's that there?

FIRST OFFICER: Immigration, open up.

Eddie turns, looks at Beatrice. She sits. Then he looks at Catherine. With a sob of fury Catherine streaks into a bedroom.

Knock is repeated.

EDDIE: All right, take it easy, take it easy. *He goes and opens the door. The Officer steps inside.* What's all this?

FIRST OFFICER: Where are they?

Second Officer sweeps past and, glancing about, goes into the kitchen.

EDDIE: Where's who?

FIRST OFFICER: Come on, come on, where are they? *He hurries into the bedrooms.*

EDDIE: Who? We got nobody here. *He looks at Beatrice, who turns her head away. Pugnaciously, furious, he steps toward Beatrice.* What's the matter with *you?*

First Officer enters from the bedroom, calls to the kitchen.

FIRST OFFICER: Dominick?

Enter Second Officer from kitchen.

SECOND OFFICER: Maybe it's a different apartment.

FIRST OFFICER: There's only two more floors up there. I'll take the front, you go up the fire escape. I'll let you in. Watch your step up there.

SECOND OFFICER: Okay, right, Charley. *First Officer goes out apartment door and runs up the stairs.* This is Four-forty-one, isn't it?

EDDIE: That's right.

Second Officer goes out into the kitchen.

Eddie turns to Beatrice. She looks at him now and sees his terror.

BEATRICE, *weakened with fear:* Oh, Jesus, Eddie.

EDDIE: What's the matter with *you?*

BEATRICE, *pressing her palms against her face:* Oh, my God, my God.

EDDIE: What're you, accusin' me?

BEATRICE—*her final thrust is to turn toward him instead of running from him:* My God, what did you do?

Many steps on the outer stair draw his attention. We see the First Officer descending, with Marco, behind him Rodolpho, and Catherine and the two strange immigrants, followed by Second Officer. Beatrice hurries to door.

CATHERINE, *backing down stairs, fighting with First Officer; as they appear on the stairs:* What do yiz want from them? They work, that's all. They're boarders upstairs, they work on the piers.

BEATRICE, *to First Officer:* Ah, Mister, what do you want from them, who do they hurt?

CATHERINE, *pointing to Rodolpho:* They ain't no submarines, he was born in Philadelphia.

FIRST OFFICER: Step aside, lady.

CATHERINE: What do you mean? You can't just come in a house and—

FIRST OFFICER: All right, take it easy. *To Rodolpho:* What street were you born in Philadelphia?

CATHERINE: What do you mean, what street? Could you tell me what street you were born?

FIRST OFFICER: Sure. Four blocks away, One-eleven Union Street. Let's go fellas.

CATHERINE, *fending him off Rodolpho:* No, you can't! Now, get outa here!

FIRST OFFICER: Look, girlie, if they're all right they'll be out tomorrow. If they're illegal they go back where they came from. If you want, get yourself a lawyer, although I'm tellin' you now you're wasting your money. Let's get them in the car, Dom. *To the men:* Andiamo, Andiamo, let's go.

The men start, but Marco hangs back.

BEATRICE, *from doorway:* Who're they hurtin', for God's sake, what do you want from them? They're starvin' over there, what do you want! Marco!

Marco suddenly breaks from the group and dashes into the

room and faces Eddie; Beatrice and First Officer rush in as Marco spits into Eddie's face.

Catherine runs into hallway and throws herself into Rodolpho's arms. Eddie, with an enraged cry, lunges for Marco.

EDDIE: Oh, you mother's—!

First Officer quickly intercedes and pushes Eddie from Marco, who stands there accusingly.

FIRST OFFICER, *between them, pushing Eddie from Marco:* Cut it out!

EDDIE, *over the First Officer's shoulder, to Marco:* I'll kill you for that, you son of a bitch!

FIRST OFFICER: Hey! *Shakes him.* Stay in here now, don't come out, don't bother him. You hear me? Don't come out, fella.

For an instant there is silence. Then First Officer turns and takes Marco's arm and then gives a last, informative look at Eddie. As he and Marco are going out into the hall, Eddie erupts.

EDDIE: I don't forget that, Marco! You hear what I'm sayin'?

Out in the hall, First Officer and Marco go down the stairs. Now, in the street, Louis, Mike, and several neighbors including the butcher, Lipari—a stout, intense, middle-aged man—are gathering around the stoop.

Lipari, the butcher, walks over to the two strange men and kisses them. His wife, keening, goes and kisses their hands. Eddie is emerging from the house shouting after Marco. Beatrice is trying to restrain him.

EDDIE: That's the thanks I get? Which I took the blankets off my bed for yiz? You gonna apologize to me, Marco! *Marco!*

FIRST OFFICER, *in the doorway with Marco:* All right, lady, let them go. Get in the car, fellas, it's right over there.

Rodolpho is almost carrying the sobbing Catherine off up the street, left.

CATHERINE: He was born in Philadelphia! What do you want from him?

FIRST OFFICER: Step aside, lady, come on now . . .

The Second Officer has moved off with the two strange men. Marco, taking advantage of the First Officer's being occupied with Catherine, suddenly frees himself and points back at Eddie.

MARCO: That one! I accuse that one!

Eddie brushes Beatrice aside and rushes out to the stoop.

FIRST OFFICER, *grabbing him and moving him quickly off up the left street:* Come on!

MARCO, *as he is taken off, pointing back at Eddie:* That one! He killed my children! That one stole the food from my children!

> *Marco is gone. The crowd has turned to Eddie.*

EDDIE, *to Lipari and wife:* He's crazy! I give them the blankets off my bed. Six months I kept them like my own brothers!

> *Lipari, the butcher, turns and starts up left with his arm around his wife.*

EDDIE: Lipari! *He follows Lipari up left.* For Christ's sake, I kept them, I give them the blankets off my bed!

> *Lipari and wife exit. Eddie turns and starts crossing down right to Louis and Mike.*

EDDIE: Louis! *Louis!*

> *Louis barely turns, then walks off and exits down right with Mike. Only Beatrice is left on the stoop. Catherine now returns, blank-eyed, from offstage and the car. Eddie calls after Louis and Mike.*

EDDIE: He's gonna take that back. He's gonna take that back or I'll kill him! You hear me? I'll kill him! I'll kill him! *He exits up street calling.*

> *There is a pause of darkness before the lights rise, on the reception room of a prison. Marco is seated; Alfieri, Catherine, and Rodolpho standing.*

ALFIERI: I'm waiting, Marco, what do you say?

RODOLPHO: Marco never hurt anybody.

ALFIERI: I can bail you out until your hearing comes up. But I'm not going to do it, you understand me? Unless I have your promise. You're an honorable man, I will believe your promise. Now what do you say?

MARCO: In my country he would be dead now. He would not live this long.

ALFIERI: All right, Rodolpho—you come with me now.

RODOLPHO: No! Please, Mister. Marco—promise the man. Please, I want you to watch the wedding. How can I be married and you're in here? Please, you're not going to do anything; you know you're not.

> *Marco is silent.*

CATHERINE, *kneeling left of Marco:* Marco, don't you understand?

He can't bail you out if you're gonna do something bad. To hell with Eddie. Nobody is gonna talk to him again if he lives to a hundred. Everybody knows you spit in his face, that's enough, isn't it? Give me the satisfaction—I want you at the wedding. You got a wife and kids, Marco. You could be workin' till the hearing comes up, instead of layin' around here.

MARCO, *to Alfieri:* I have no chance?

ALFIERI *crosses to behind Marco:* No, Marco. You're going back. The hearing is a formality, that's all.

MARCO: But him? There is a chance, eh?

ALFIERI: When she marries him he can start to become an American. They permit that, if the wife is born here.

MARCO, *looking at Rodolpho:* Well—we did something. *He lays a palm on Rodolpho's arm and Rodolpho covers it.*

RODOLPHO: Marco, tell the man.

MARCO, *pulling his hand away:* What will I tell him? He knows such a promise is dishonorable.

ALFIERI: To promise not to kill is not dishonorable.

MARCO, *looking at Alfieri:* No?

ALFIERI: No.

MARCO, *gesturing with his head—this is a new idea:* Then what is done with such a man?

ALFIERI: Nothing. If he obeys the law, he lives. That's all.

MARCO, *rises, turns to Alfieri:* The law? All the law is not in a book.

ALFIERI: Yes. In a book. There is no other law.

MARCO, *his anger rising:* He degraded my brother. My blood. He robbed my children, he mocks my work. I work to come here, mister!

ALFIERI: I know, Marco—

MARCO: There is no law for that? Where is the law for that?

ALFIERI: There is none.

MARCO, *shaking his head, sitting:* I don't understand this country.

ALFIERI: Well? What is your answer? You have five or six weeks you could work. Or else you sit here. What do you say to me?

MARCO *lowers his eyes. It almost seems he is ashamed.* All right.

ALFIERI: You won't touch him. This is your promise.

   Slight pause.

MARCO: Maybe he wants to apologize to me.

Marco is staring away. Alfieri takes one of his hands.

ALFIERI: This is not God, Marco. You hear? Only God makes justice.

MARCO: All right.

ALFIERI, *nodding, not with assurance:* Good! Catherine, Rodolpho, Marco, let us go.

Catherine kisses Rodolpho and Marco, then kisses Alfieri's hand.

CATHERINE: I'll get Beatrice and meet you at the church. *She leaves quickly.*

Marco rises. Rodolpho suddenly embraces him. Marco pats him on the back and Rodolpho exits after Catherine. Marco faces Alfieri.

ALFIERI: Only God, Marco.

Marco turns and walks out. Alfieri with a certain processional tread leaves the stage. The lights dim out.

The lights rise in the apartment. Eddie is alone in the rocker, rocking back and forth in little surges. Pause. Now Beatrice emerges from a bedroom. She is in her best clothes, wearing a hat.

BEATRICE, *with fear, going to Eddie:* I'll be back in about an hour, Eddie. All right?

EDDIE, *quietly, almost inaudibly, as though drained:* What, have I been talkin' to myself?

BEATRICE: Eddie, for God's sake, it's her wedding.

EDDIE: Didn't you hear what I told you? You walk out that door to that wedding you ain't comin' back here, Beatrice.

BEATRICE: Why! What do you want?

EDDIE: I want my respect. Didn't you ever hear of that? From my wife?

Catherine enters from bedroom.

CATHERINE: It's after three; we're supposed to be there already, Beatrice. The priest won't wait.

BEATRICE: Eddie. It's her wedding. There'll be nobody there from her family. For my sister let me go. I'm goin' for my sister.

EDDIE, *as though hurt:* Look, I been arguin' with you all day already, Beatrice, and I said what I'm gonna say. He's gonna come here and apologize to me or nobody from this house is goin' into that church today. Now if that's more to you than I am, then go. But don't come back. You be on my side or on their side, that's all.

CATHERINE, *suddenly:* Who the hell do you think you are?

BEATRICE: Sssh!

CATHERINE: You got no more right to tell nobody nothin'! Nobody! The rest of your life, nobody!

BEATRICE: Shut up, Katie! *She turns Catherine around.*

CATHERINE: You're gonna come with me!

BEATRICE: I can't Katie, I can't . . .

CATHERINE: How can you listen to him? This rat!

BEATRICE, *shaking Catherine:* Don't you call him that!

CATHERINE, *clearing from Beatrice:* What're you scared of? He's a rat! He belongs in the sewer!

BEATRICE: Stop it!

CATHERINE, *weeping:* He bites people when they sleep! He comes when nobody's lookin' and poisons decent people. In the garbage he belongs!

Eddie seems about to pick up the table and fling it at her.

BEATRICE: No, Eddie! Eddie! *To Catherine:* Then we all belong in the garbage. You, and me too. Don't say that. Whatever happened we all done it, and don't you ever forget it, Catherine. *She goes to Catherine.* Now go, go to your wedding, Katie, I'll stay home. Go. God bless you, God bless your children.

Enter Rodolpho.

RODOLPHO: Eddie?

EDDIE: Who said you could come in here? Get outa here!

RODOLPHO: Marco is coming, Eddie. *Pause. Beatrice raises her hands in terror.* He's praying in the church. You understand? *Pause. Rodolpho advances into the room.* Catherine, I think it is better we go. Come with me.

CATHERINE: Eddie go away please.

BEATRICE, *quietly:* Eddie. Let's go someplace. Come. You and me. *He has not moved.* I don't want you to be here when he comes. I'll get your coat.

EDDIE: Where? Where am I goin'? This is my house.

BEATRICE, *crying out:* What's the use of it! He's crazy now, you know the way they get, what good is it! You got nothin' against Marco, you always liked Marco!

EDDIE: I got nothin' against Marco? Which he called me a rat in front of the whole neighborhood? Which he said I killed his children! Where you been?

RODOLPHO, *quite suddenly, stepping up to Eddie:* It is my fault, Eddie. Everything. I wish to apologize. It was wrong that I do not ask your permission. I kiss your hand. *He reaches for Eddie's hand, but Eddie snaps it away from him.*

BEATRICE: Eddie, he's apologizing!

RODOLPHO: I have made all our troubles. But you have insult me too. Maybe God understand why you did that to me. Maybe you did not mean to insult me at all—

BEATRICE: Listen to him! Eddie, listen what he's tellin' you!

RODOLPHO: I think, maybe when Marco comes, if we can tell him we are comrades now, and we have no more argument between us. Then maybe Marco will not—

EDDIE: Now, listen—

CATHERINE: Eddie, give him a chance!

BEATRICE: What do you want! Eddie, what do you want!

EDDIE: I want my name! He didn't take my name; he's only a punk. Marco's got my name—*to Rodolpho:* and you can run tell him, kid, that he's gonna give it back to me in front of this neighborhood, or we have it out. *Hoisting up his pants:* Come on, where is he? Take me to him.

BEATRICE: Eddie, listen—

EDDIE: I heard enough! Come on, let's go!

BEATRICE: Only blood is good? He kissed your hand!

EDDIE: What he does don't mean nothin' to nobody! *To Rodolpho:* Come on!

BEATRICE, *barring his way to the stairs:* What's gonna mean somethin'? Eddie, listen to me. Who could give you your name? Listen to me, I love you, I'm talkin' to you, I love you; if Marco'll kiss your hand outside, if he goes on his knees, what is he got to give you? That's not what you want.

EDDIE: Don't bother me!

BEATRICE: You want somethin' else, Eddie, and you can never have her!

CATHERINE, *in horror:* B.!

EDDIE, *shocked, horrified, his fists clenching:* Beatrice!

Marco appears outside, walking toward the door from a distant point.

BEATRICE, *crying out, weeping:* The truth is not as bad as blood, Eddie! I'm tellin' you the truth—tell her good-by forever!

EDDIE, *crying out in agony:* That's what you think of me—that I would have such a thoughts? *His fists clench his head as though it will burst.*

MARCO, *calling near the door outside:* Eddie Carbone!

Eddie swerves about; all stand transfixed for an instant. People appear outside.

EDDIE, *as though flinging his challenge:* Yeah, Marco! Eddie Carbone. Eddie Carbone. Eddie Carbone. *He goes up the stairs and emerges from the apartment. Rodolpho streaks up and out past him and runs to Marco.*

RODOLPHO: No, Marco, please! Eddie, please, he has children! You will kill a family!

BEATRICE: Go in the house! Eddie, go in the house!

EDDIE—*he gradually comes to address the people:* Maybe he come to apologize to me. Heh, Marco? For what you said about me in front of the neighborhood? *He is incensing himself and little bits of laughter even escape him as his eyes are murderous and he cracks his knuckles in his hands with a strange sort of relaxation.* He knows that ain't right. To do like that? To a man? Which I put my roof over their head and my food in their mouth? Like in the Bible? Strangers I never seen in my whole life? To come out of the water and grab a girl for a passport? To go and take from your own family like from the stable—and never a word to me? And now accusations in the bargain! *Directly to Marco:* Wipin' the neighborhood with my name like a dirty rag! I want my name, Marco. *He is moving now, carefully, toward Marco.* Now gimme my name and we go together to the wedding.

BEATRICE and CATHERINE, *keening:* Eddie! Eddie, don't! Eddie!

EDDIE: No, Marco knows what's right from wrong. Tell the people, Marco, tell them what a liar you are! *He has his arms spread and Marco is spreading his.* Come on, liar, you know what you done! *He lunges for Marco as a great hushed shout goes up from the people.*

Marco strikes Eddie beside the neck.

MARCO: Animal! You go on your knees to me!

Eddie goes down with the blow and Marco starts to raise a foot to stomp him when Eddie springs a knife into his hand and Marco steps back. Louis rushes in toward Eddie.

LOUIS: Eddie, for Christ's sake!

Eddie raises the knife and Louis halts and steps back.

EDDIE: You lied about me, Marco. Now say it. Come on now, say it!

MARCO: Anima-a-a-l!

Eddie lunges with the knife. Marco grabs his arm, turning the blade inward and pressing it home as the women and Louis and Mike rush in and separate them, and Eddie, the knife still in his hand, falls to his knees before Marco. The two women support him for a moment, calling his name again and again.

CATHERINE: Eddie I never meant to do nothing bad to you.

EDDIE: Then why— Oh, B.!

BEATRICE: Yes, yes!

EDDIE: My B.!

He dies in her arms, and Beatrice covers him with her body. Alfieri, who is in the crowd, turns out to the audience. The lights have gone down, leaving him in a glow, while behind him the dull prayers of the people and the keening of the women continue.

ALFIERI: Most of the time now we settle for half and I like it better. But the truth is holy, and even as I know how wrong he was, and his death useless, I tremble, for I confess that something perversely pure calls to me from his memory—not purely good, but himself purely, for he allowed himself to be wholly known and for that I think I will love him more than all my sensible clients. And yet, it is better to settle for half, it must be! And so I mourn him—I admit it—with a certain . . . alarm.

CURTAIN